Programming in Ada®: a first course

® Ada is a registered trademark of
the Ada Joint Program
US Government

Programming in Ada

A FIRST COURSE

ROBERT G. CLARK
Department of Computing Science, University of Stirling

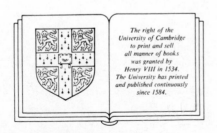

The right of the
University of Cambridge
to print and sell
all manner of books
was granted by
Henry VIII in 1534.
The University has printed
and published continuously
since 1584.

CAMBRIDGE UNIVERSITY PRESS
Cambridge
London New York New Rochelle
Melbourne Sydney

Published by the Press Syndicate of the University of Cambridge
The Pitt Building, Trumpington Street, Cambridge CB2 1RP
32 East 57th Street, New York, NY 10022, USA
10 Stamford Road, Oakleigh, Melbourne 3166, Australia

© Cambridge University Press 1985

First published 1985

Printed in Great Britain at the University Press, Cambridge

Library of Congress catalogue card number: 84-14965

British Library cataloguing in publication data
Clark, Robert G.
    Programming in Ada : a first course.
    1. Ada (Computer program language)
    I. Title.
    001.64'24   QA76.73.A15
    ISBN 0 521 25728 X hard covers
    ISBN 0 521 27675 6 paperback

CONTENTS

PREFACE

This book is intended for students who are taking a first course in computer programming at college or university. Little or no knowledge of programming is assumed, although the book may be used to give a gentle introduction to Ada for those with some experience of languages such as Pascal or Fortran.

Writing reliable programs is not easy. Solutions to problems must be designed systematically before they can be implemented on a computer. The main aim of this book is to show how to design and write computer programs which are reliable, easy to understand and reasonably efficient. A second aim of the book is to give an introduction to the Ada programming language.

At present Pascal is the main language used in introductory courses. Ada was developed from Pascal and, although it is a much larger language, I believe that a suitably chosen subset of Ada gives the better introduction to programming concepts. The single most important feature of a modern language is that it should promote reliability. The package concept of Ada is a major tool in the development of reliable programs and is missing from languages such as Pascal. If a student's initial course in problem solving on a computer does not involve packages or their equivalent, then these will be seen as a foreign and difficult concept rather than an obvious way of tackling many problems.

The increasing cost and concern about the reliability of computer software has been described as the 'software crisis'. In 1975, in response to this, the US Government drew up a list of requirements which they wanted to see in a language. When no existing language met these requirements, they decided to invite proposals for the design of a new language. This international competition was won in 1979 by a team from CII Honeywell Bull headed by Jean Ichbiah. The new language was called Ada in honour of Augusta Ada, Countess of Lovelace. She was the daughter of Lord Byron and her work with the nineteenth-century computer pioneer Charles Babbage meant that she can be considered as the world's first computer programmer.

The initial version of the Ada Language Reference Manual was published in 1980, but since then the language has undergone several revisions. The language described in this book is the final version (ANSI/MIL-STD-1815A-1983).

Ada is a very large language and no attempt is made in this book to cover it all. Instead the emphasis is on the development of a good programming style. The early parts of the book concentrate on solving small problems and introducing the language features necessary to write small programs. The description of type and object declarations has been simplified, but this has been done in a way which does not reduce the power of the language. The later parts of the book show how packages can be used in constructing large reliable programs and their use in information hiding and in the definition of abstract data types. The last few chapters cover separate compilation, exceptions and files. Generics, access types and tasks are not covered.

Throughout the book solutions to problems are developed by means of stepwise refinement to give complete Ada programs. All the programs were tested first using the University of York Ada compiler and then using the validated Data General/ROLM compiler. In the tests using the ROLM compiler, package *text_io* was used throughout with type *real* defined as

    type *real* **is digits** 6;

Packages *int_io* and *real_io* were instantiated as described in appendix 2. I would like to thank Iain Richmond of the Edinburgh Regional Computing Centre for his help in arranging these tests.

I would also like to thank my colleagues Charles Rattray and Dave Budgen in the Computing Science Department of Stirling University for their helpful comments. Last, but not least, I would like to thank my wife and children for their patience while the book was being written.

    Robert G Clark
    Stirling, December 1984

1

Problem solving with computers

1.1 Introduction

This book is about solving problems using a computer. A major aim is to describe how we can systematically design solutions to problems and how we can then implement these solutions on a computer. The result should be computer programs which can be easily understood and are straightforward, reliable and reasonably efficient.

The programs are going to be written in a language called Ada, which is well suited to this approach to problem solving. The second major aim of the book is to give an introduction to the Ada language. No previous knowledge of Ada or any other programming language is assumed, although it is expected that many readers will have had some experience with computers in school or elsewhere.

As they are used in so many different areas, most people have some idea of what computers can do, but they may not be at all sure how they manage to do it. To clear up any misconceptions, it will be useful to have a simple definition of a computer:

> A computer is an electronic machine which can be given, and which will then obey, a series of instructions.

It is important to realise that before a computer can carry out a task such as sending you an electricity bill or playing chess, it must have been given precise and unambiguous instructions of what to do. To be understandable to the computer, the instructions must have been written in some language which the computer can understand. A set of instructions informing a computer how to carry out some task is called a program.

If we want to use a computer to solve a problem, we do not just sit down and write a program. We must first make sure that we fully understand what the problem is and we must then *design* a suitable solution. Only after this has been done do we start writing the actual program, in some suitable language. The act of programming is concerned with program design and not just with writing programs. We shall discover that problem specification and the design of solutions is much more difficult than implementing a solution in some programming language.

Before we look at how we go about designing programs, let us briefly consider the components which go to make up a computer system.

1.2 **The computer**

Although computers vary greatly in size, power and cost, from a home computer owned by an amateur enthusiast to a machine supporting the data processing functions of a large company, they all consist of the same basic components.

1. *A main store*

   This is where both program instructions and the data to be used by the instructions are held. Before instructions can be obeyed by a computer they must have been loaded into the computer's main store. When the instructions in a program are being obeyed by a computer, we say that the program is being run or is being executed.

2. *A central processing unit (CPU)*

   This is the unit which actually carries out the instructions. Each instruction is very simple; it may be something like adding two numbers together. The power of the computer is the speed at which it can carry out instructions (hundreds of thousands each second) and quickly performing a series of simple operations can be equivalent to carrying out a very complex task.

3. *Backing store*

   Programs and data which are not immediately required can be held on what is known as the backing store. This usually consists of magnetic tape or disks and in general much more information can be held there than can be held in the main store. For this reason the backing store is used for the long-term storage of programs and data. The backing store can be regarded as a large filing system with information such as programs being filed away in individual files. Program instructions must be copied from their file on backing store and loaded into the main store before they can be obeyed.

4. *Input and output devices*

An input device is used to read information into a computer and the results of running a program are presented to the user by an output device. The most common device is the interactive terminal, which can act both as an input and as an output device. It usually consists of a screen (like a television screen) and a typewriter keyboard and is often referred to as a visual display unit or VDU. Information can be typed in at the keyboard and both the information typed in and the results produced by the program are displayed on the screen. In this way the user can interact with the running of a program. Another output device is the printer, which can be used to print out results so that they can be taken away for further study.

The main store, CPU, backing store and the input and output devices are together known as the computer hardware. Programs, on the other hand, are what is known as computer software.

1.3 Computer software

Whenever we use a computer to run a program, we find that it has already been loaded with a set of programs whose job is to help us. This set of programs is called the computer operating system. The computer as seen by the user is the computer hardware plus the operating system. It is convenient to consider the two together and not worry about what is done by the hardware and what is done by the operating system software. We shall refer to their combined effect as the computer system.

There is one problem which we have not yet considered. Each computer can undertand only one language, called its machine language. Because such languages are very difficult for human beings to understand we do not write programs in machine language, but write them instead in languages that have been specially designed to be easier to use. Examples of such languages, called high-level languages, are Fortran, Cobol, Pascal and Ada.

For a computer to understand a program written in a high-level language, the program must first be translated into the machine's own language. Available with the operating system we must therefore have specially written translating programs. They are called compilers. To be able to run programs written in Fortran on a computer system we must have a Fortran compiler, to be able to run programs written in

Pascal we must have a Pascal compiler and to be able to run programs written in Ada, we must have an Ada compiler.

This may appear to be a major disadvantage in using high-level languages, but it in fact leads to a major advantage. It should be possible to run a program written in Ada for example on any computer that has an Ada compiler. For this reason such languages are said to be machine-independent. In practice this is not quite as good as it sounds: different versions of most programming languages exist and the characteristics of different machines often mean that programs written for one machine cannot be run on another. The designers of Ada have tackled this problem by strictly defining the language and not allowing dialects. It is also possible to keep features that may be machine-dependent separate from the rest of an Ada program. The aim of being able to write Ada programs for one machine and have them able to be run on all machines that have an Ada compiler should be realisable.

Having to have a program written in a high-level language translated before it can be run has another advantage. Programming languages are just like ordinary languages and have grammatical rules which tell us what is allowed and what is not. If we have made any grammatical mistakes in writing a program, they will be picked up and reported to us during the translation process. These mistakes, known as syntax errors or compile-time errors, can then be corrected by the programmer before another attempt is made to translate the program.

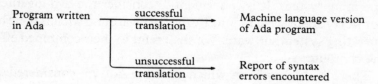

Note that it is not the program written in Ada but a machine language version of it which is eventually executed. Nevertheless, when considering the execution of a program, it is useful to continue to think in terms of the original Ada program. Errors, called run-time errors, can occur during execution and when the computer system picks up a run-time error it may stop the execution of the offending program. It should then give a helpful message to inform us of what has gone wrong. This message should be expressed in terms of the original Ada program, so that it can be understood by programmers with knowledge of Ada but with little or no knowledge of machine language or the structure of a particular computer.

Even when a program runs successfully to completion there is no guarantee that its results are correct, for there may be logical errors in the attempted solution. Testing programs with carefully chosen test data is therefore very important. Finding and correcting errors in this way is called "debugging".

You will find that compile-time errors are much easier to find and correct than run-time errors, which are much easier to find and correct than logical errors. Ada has been designed so that as many errors as possible are picked up at compile-time. Moreover some logical errors, which would remain undetected in programs written in many other languages, will cause run-time errors to be produced.

1.4 Stepwise refinement

Let us now consider how we can go about solving a problem. As has already been said, there are several important steps which must be taken before we can start writing the actual program.

With complex problems finding out exactly what is required is crucial and can be the most difficult part of the whole process. Any mistakes made at this stage can be very expensive, as they will lead to the wrong problem being solved. This step does not play a large part in this book because the problems which we shall consider will already be fairly well defined. It is, however, important to remember the importance of this first step when problems in commerce, industry and research are being dealt with.

Learning how to design the solutions to problems does play an important part in this book. A way of solving a problem is called an algorithm, which can be defined as

> an unambiguous sequence of instructions which, when followed, gives the required result in a finite time.

We are therefore interested in designing algorithms. Let us look at this through an example problem, such as that of finding the sum of the squares of all the odd numbers from 1 to 99.

It is often best to start by forgetting about the computer and to consider how we might go about tackling a problem with pencil and paper. Our approach would most likely be to take each of the odd numbers in turn, calculate its square and add this value to some running total. This gives us the basis of our computer solution, which we can write informally as

> set running total to zero
> take each odd number in the range 1 to 99 in turn and add its
>   square to the running total
> write down the final value of the running total

This outline solution has ignored details such as how the sequence of odd numbers is to be produced. Our next step is to expand the outline solution to indicate how we are going to produce each of the odd numbers in turn. A possible method is to start with the first odd number and to always generate the next odd number by adding two to the current one. Our algorithm then becomes

> set running total to zero
> set odd number to one
> loop while the odd number is less than or equal to 99
>   add the square of the current odd number to the running total
>   add two to the current odd number
> end loop
> write the final value of the running total

The idea is that the instructions between the words "loop" and "end loop" are executed with each of the odd numbers between 1 and 99 in turn.

This approach to problem solving is called programming by stepwise refinement. We first produce an outline solution which does not go into detail. This solution is then expanded or refined in a stepwise manner until it contains sufficient detail for us to be able to implement it in some programming language. The outline solution and its refinements are written in a restricted form of English so that the design is not dependent on the features of a particular programming language.

As this is a fairly simple problem, we are now in a position to write the computer program. Provided the design stage has been done properly, producing the program in Ada or some other language is relatively straightforward. The principal intellectual challenge is in producing the design, not in implementing the design in a programming language.

So that we can see what a complete Ada program looks like, a program corresponding to this design is given below. Do not worry about following all the details; they are explained in the next few chapters. The important thing to note is how closely the Ada program follows our informal design in English and how, even with no knowledge of Ada, it is possible for you to have a fair idea of what the program is doing.

PROGRAM 1.1

```
with student_io; use student_io;
procedure odd_square is
    sum_odd : integer := 0;
    odd_number : integer := 1;
begin
    --find the sum of the squares of the odd numbers from 1 to 99
    while odd_number < = 99 loop
        sum_odd := sum_odd + odd_number * odd_number;
        odd_number := odd_number + 2;
        --sum_odd contains the sum of the squares so far
    end loop;
    put("The sum of the odd number is ");
    put(sum_odd); new_line;
end odd_square;
```

One important question has remained unanswered. Once we have designed and written a small Ada program, how do we get it into the computer? The exact answer depends on the computer system you are using, but it is likely that the following approach will be used.

One of the programs available with the operating system will be an editor. This is used both to put new information (such as a program) into the computer and to modify or edit existing information. Using the editor to control things, we can type an Ada program in at a computer terminal. Once we have finished typing it in the editor will put it into a file on backing store.

Precise details of how to use the editor depends on the particular system you are using and is outside the scope of this book.

Once our Ada program is in a file, we can attempt to translate it using the Ada compiler. If the translation is successful a new file containing the machine code version of the program will be created. If the translation is not successful we shall be given a list of error messages. We can then use the editor to modify our original program to produce a new corrected version and attempt to have it translated.

The program we developed in this section was very simple. In the next section we consider some of the extra difficulties which arise when very large problems are to be solved.

1.5 Constructing large programs

Programs written to solve complex tasks can be very large and very complicated. Because computers are used for such diverse purposes as controlling nuclear power stations and maintaining records of deposits and withdrawals in bank accounts, it is vital that the programs controlling these functions always work correctly.

The difficulty and cost of producing large complex systems which did not frequently break down was not always recognised and this eventually led to a crisis in the software industry. This in turn sparked off a great deal of research on how we should go about constructing large systems. The subject of how to produce high quality, reliable and cost-effective software is called software engineering.

When we first learn how to program, we practise our skills by writing small programs which are usually thrown away once we have managed to get them to work. Problems concerned with complex systems on the other hand require programs which are too large to be written by a single person and need instead to be written by groups of programmers. Moreover, the resulting programs may be used for many years and, as it is common for the requirements of the system to be changed during this time, modifications have to be made to the programs. These modifications will usually be made by different programmers from those who produced the original.

It is now generally recognised that the first priority in producing programs which will be reliable and can be easily modified is that they should be straightforward and easily understood. The question of how to do this has been widely studied and the structure of the Ada language follows the latest thinking in this field.

The problem of program size is best tackled by attempting to break large problems into a series of relatively self-contained subproblems which can be solved independently. Each subproblem is then further divided into a series of yet simpler problems. We continue in this way until each of the subproblems is so simple that its solution can be easily written down.

The kinds of problems we encounter when we start programming are often the subproblems which experienced programmers generate when solving large problems. The solution to small problems is therefore approached in the same way as the solution to large ones; that is, we divide them into a series of yet smaller problems. This is the approach described in the previous section, but viewed from a different angle. The first part of this book deals with how we can go about constructing small programs. The basic features of the Ada language are introduced, but no attempt is made to cover all aspects of what is a very large language.

The Ada package is then introduced. It is the mechanism which enables us to produce large systems without being overwhelmed by their size. Packages allow the solution to a subproblem to be designed, implemented and tested separately from the rest of the program. Once the solutions to the different subproblems have been shown to work they can be joined together to form the final program. Even after this has been done, parts of a program can be modified and the changes tested without the other parts, which remain unchanged, being affected.

After we have divided a problem into a series of subproblems we may find that packages to solve one or more of the subproblems have already been written. Instead of attempting to re-invent the wheel, we can make use of these packages. Most Ada implementations will have large libraries of such useful solutions, allowing us to build on what other people have done rather than always having to start from scratch with each new program.

We shall return to these topics once we know something about the Ada language.

2

Ada programs

2.1 A complete Ada program

Before we go any further let us examine the structure of a simple Ada program in some detail.

PROGRAM 2.1

```
with student_io; use student_io;
procedure add is
    first, second, sum : integer;
begin
    --program to print the sum of two integers
    first := 94;
    second := 127;
    sum := first + second;
    put("Sum =");
    put(sum);
    new_line;
end add;
```

This program will calculate and then print out the sum of the two numbers 94 and 127.

The first line of the program

   with *student_io*; **use** *student_io*;

is what is known as a context clause. It makes lots of helpful routines available to us and should just be taken on trust here. Exactly what it does will be explained later.

Note that in the program the words **with, use, procedure, is, begin** and **end** are in bold type. They are called reserved words and are part of the Ada language. They are in bold type so that they stand out and help make the structure of the program clear, but they are not typed in any special way in the version presented to the computer. Other reserved words will be introduced later, and a complete list is given in appendix 1.

A simple Ada program consists of what is called a procedure and the second line of our program

procedure *add* **is**

introduces the procedure and gives it the name *add*. The choice of names is left up to the programmer, but it is always good practice to choose names which help to explain what is happening in a program. In programming, names are referred to as identifiers.

The third line

first, second, sum : integer;

is called the declarative part of the procedure. In it three variable objects are introduced or declared and are given names (*first, second* and *sum*) so that they can be referred to later in the program. Variable objects, or variables, are used in programming languages to store, or hold, values. They are called variables because during the execution of a program the values which they store may be changed many times.

A variable object is restricted to being able to store values of only one particular kind or type. In this declaration the three variables are declared to be of type *integer*. This means that the variable objects *first, second* and *sum* can only be used to store values which are whole numbers. We refer to them as integer variables.

The type of a variable determines both the range of values which it may hold and the kind of operations in which it may become involved. Ada has several built-in types, such as *integer* and *float*. Integer variables can be used in the arithmetic operations of addition, subtraction, multiplication, division, etc. As we shall see later, float variables are used to store fractional numerical values and can also be used in arithmetic operations.

A variable object therefore has a name, a value and a type. The name and type are fixed when the variable is declared, but its value may change during execution of the program.

Let us now look at the effect of executing the Ada program. Programs are executed by obeying in turn the sequence of instructions or statements between the reserved words **begin** and **end**.

Immediately following the **begin** we have a comment:

--program to print the sum of two integers

Comments are introduced by two consecutive hyphens and are terminated by the end of a line. They exist purely to help the human reader and are ignored by a computer during the execution of the program.

The first two statements in the program are

> *first* := 94;
> *second* := 127;

They are called assignment statements and are the means by which values can be stored in variables. The composite symbol ":=" should be read as "takes the value of".

The effect of executing these two statements is to store the integer value 94 in the variable called *first* and the integer value 127 in the variable called *second*. We say that the variables *first* and *second* have been assigned the values 94 and 127 respectively.

The next statement

> *sum* := *first* + *second*;

causes the value of the variable *first* to be added to the value of the variable *second* and the resulting value to be assigned to the variable *sum*.

The statement

> *put*("Sum =");

is called an output statement and it causes the message

> Sum =

to be written out. In programming, a series of characters surrounded by quotation characters is called a string.

This is followed by another output statement

> *put*(*sum*);

which causes the value of the variable *sum* to be written out. Note the difference between these two statements. In the first we wanted the actual series of characters to be written out and so we enclosed them in quotation characters. In the second the value of a variable is printed. The combined effect of these two statements is to write out

> Sum =   221

Successive output statements cause information to be written on the same line. To go on to a new line requires the statement

> *new_line*;

This is the last of the sequence of statements and execution of the program stops after it has been obeyed.

In the last line of the program, the name of the procedure is again given after the reserved word **end**. This is not essential in Ada, but is strongly recommended so that when people read an Ada program it is clear to them where a procedure begins and where it ends.

A simple Ada program therefore consists of two parts. Between the reserved words **is** and **begin** we have the declarations where the identifiers which are to be used in the rest of the program are introduced. Between **begin** and **end** we have a list of statements with each statement being terminated by a semi-colon. The program is executed by obeying the statements one after the other.

2.2 Programs with input data

Program 2.1 is not very flexible in that it can only be used to find the sum of 94 and 127. A more useful program would be one which could read in two integer values and write out their sum. This is shown below.

PROGRAM 2.2

```
with student_io; use student_io;
procedure add_any is
    first, second, sum : integer;
begin
    --program to read two integers and
    --to print their sum
    put("two whole numbers please:");
    get(first); get(second);
    sum := first + second;
    put("Sum =");
    put(sum);
    new_line;
end add_any;
```

This program involves the user in interacting with the execution of the program. The user must type in information before an answer can be calculated and printed out. In this and in the other examples we assume that the programs are being run at an interactive terminal.

Let us now look at what is involved.

Three integer variables *first*, *second* and *sum* have again been declared. The first statement to be executed in the program is now

   put("two whole numbers please:");

which will cause the message

   two whole numbers please:

to be written out.

The reason for this instruction is to give a message or prompt to the person running the program that they should now type in two integer numbers. This is because the next two statements in the program, *get(first); get(second);*

are input statements and require two integers to be typed in as data. Once they have been typed in, the two numbers are read by the program and stored in the variables *first* and *second* respectively.

The statement

sum := first + second;

assigns the sum of the two values to *sum* as before. The answer is then printed out, along with a suitable explanatory message, by the statements

put("Sum =");
put(*sum*);
new_line;

As we have now come to the end of the sequence of statements, execution of the program stops.

2.3 Comments and program layout

When writing programs it is very important to remember that they have to be read and understood by human beings as well as by computers. It is therefore important always to choose meaningful identifiers and to lay out a program well so that its structure is clear.

In Programs 2.1 and 2.2 for example, the sequence of statements between **begin** and **end** is indented. This helps to show where the sequence starts and where it finishes. The examples in the book should be used as a guide to a suitable layout for Ada programs. For example, we normally write each statement on a separate line unless they are very simple and are related to one another.

The layout of a program does not affect its meaning, although identifiers, reserved words and numbers must always be separated from one another by at least one space or by taking a new line. Several spaces or new lines can always be used wherever one space is allowed.

Comments can be used to help clarify the meaning of a program. Comments start with two consecutive hyphens and are terminated by the end of the line. They have no effect on the meaning of a program, but are solely for the benefit of human readers.

It is always useful to put a comment at the beginning of each procedure to describe its intended effect. The comment in Program 2.1

--program to print the sum of two integers

is used in this way. Other comments should be used to explain difficult or critical parts of a program.

2.4 Syntax diagrams

We have now seen what an Ada program looks like, but before we look in detail at the language it will be useful for us to have a simple notation in which the language can be described. The rules which govern what is, and what is not, a valid program are called the syntax rules. It is possible to describe these rules informally in English.

We have seen, for example, that names are represented by what are called identifiers. Although we have used identifiers in Programs 2.1 and 2.2, we have not yet strictly defined them.

An identifier can be defined, in English, by the following syntax rule:

> An identifier is a letter followed by zero or more letters or digits. An optional underline character can appear between any two letters or digits.

Examples of identifiers are

    x
    first_case
    Julia
    Chapter_2

As definitions in English are rather long and can be ambiguous, a better way of describing the syntax rules is to use syntax diagrams. The syntax diagram for an identifier is

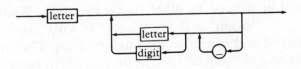

All possible paths through this diagram describe a valid Ada identifier. We therefore have an equivalent definition of an identifier to the one given earlier in English.

In syntax diagrams, items in rounded boxes or circles such as the underline character "_" actually appear in Ada programs while items in rectangular boxes describe the kind of item which is to appear.

Items in rectangular boxes must be defined by further syntax diagrams. A digit, for example, is defined by

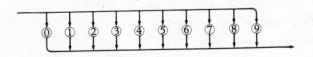

This shows that a digit is one of the characters "0", "1", "2", "3", "4", "5", "6", "7", "8" or "9". A letter is one of the 26 upper or 26 lower case letters.

Identifiers which differ only in the use of corresponding upper and lower case letters are considered to be the same. Hence

Same   same   SAME   sAMe

are all equivalent ways of writing the identifier "same".

As a further example of a syntax diagram let us now look at the structure of a simple Ada program.

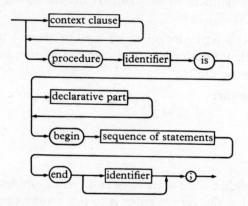

Because they are in rectangular boxes, what exactly is meant by "context clause", "identifier", "declarative part" and "sequence of statements" will be defined by other syntax diagrams. Words like "procedure", "is", "begin" and "end", on the other hand, are in rounded boxes and will appear in the final program. They are the reserved words and may not be used as ordinary identifiers.

Exercises

1. Which of the following are valid Ada identifiers?

   total   Total   sum_1   sum1   sum__1   sum_1.5
   SECOND   begin   _average   "final"   TotalCount
   Total_Count   2nd   Begin   END

2. Which identifiers in question 1 have we encountered as reserved words?

3. Define the terms "variable" and "type".

4. In response to the prompt

   two whole numbers please:

a user types in

   15 28

as data for Program 2.2. What will be printed out by the program in response?

5. Why is it important for a program to be laid out well and for it to contain explanatory comments?

6. Write a program which will read two integers and print the result of subtracting the first from the second.

(Answers to selected exercises are given at the end of the book.)

3

Types and values

3.1 Variable object declarations

In chapter 2 we used the declaration

first, second, sum : integer;

to declare three integer variables called *first*, *second* and *sum*. As we have seen, a variable has a name and a type and is used to store a value. Variable objects are created by being declared and this gives them their name and type.

The type of a variable determines the range of values which it may hold and the kind of operations in which it may become involved. In the above example the variables are declared to be of the built-in type *integer*.

Programs 2.1 and 2.2 both have a single declaration in their declarative part, but more than one declaration, or indeed no declarations at all, is perfectly acceptable. It is even possible to split our earlier declarations into three without changing the meaning in any way.

first : integer;
second : integer;
sum : integer;

As well as being given a name and a type, variables may be given an initial value when they are declared. Hence in the object declarations

table_size : integer : = 20;
maximum, minimum : integer : = 0;

the integer variable *table_size* is created and given the initial value 20 and the integer variables *maximum* and *minimum* are created and given the initial value 0.

If a variable is not given a value when it is declared, as was the case in our earlier examples, then we say that its value is undefined. It remains undefined until the variable is given a value in an assignment or input statement. Because it would not make any sense, it is wrong to attempt to refer to the value of a variable which is undefined. Variables which have been given an initial value can have that value changed later in the program.

3.2 Constant object declarations

It is fairly common for the same constant value to appear several times in a program. A program might, for example, be dealing with groups of 50 people and so the number 50 may appear more than once. A person reading the program might not be sure whether these different occurrences are coincidental or whether they all refer to the same thing and must be the same. As well as variable objects it is therefore possible to declare constant objects in an Ada program. We can have

group_size: **constant** *integer* := 50;

This causes a constant integer object called *group_size* to be created and given the value 50.

Now, instead of using the anonymous value 50 for the size of the groups, we can use the constant identifier *group_size*. If, by coincidence, the number 50 was required in the program for some other purpose we would not use the identifier *group_size* to refer to it.

Constant objects differ from variable objects in that they must be given an initial value when they are declared and that value may not be changed later in the program.

Using constant identifiers has several other advantages. If we wished to modify the program so that it could now deal with groups of 60 people all we would have to do is change the constant declaration to

group_size: **constant** *integer* := 60;

instead of searching through the program for the different occurrences of the number 50.

Perhaps an even more important reason for having constant identifiers is that using meaningful identifiers for significant constants in a program also makes a program easier to understand. If, for example, a program was dealing with the number of days in a week it would be better to use the constant identifier that was declared as

days_in_week: **constant** *integer* := 7;

rather than simply use the number 7.

The following program, which is used to calculate an employee's wages, contains two constant identifiers – one representing the ordinary rate of pay and the other the overtime rate. The program requires two integer numbers to be typed in as data, the first to represent the total number of hours worked and the second the number of hours of overtime worked by an employee and, using this information, it calculates and prints out the employee's wages.

PROGRAM 3.1

```
with student_io; use student_io;
procedure wages is
    total_hours, overtime, normal : integer; --hours worked
    pay, basic_pay, overtime_pay : integer;
    rate_of_pay : constant integer := 8; -- hourly $ rate
    overtime_rate: constant integer := 12;
begin
    --program to read hours worked and calculate pay
    put("Total number of hours worked is ");
    get(total_hours);
    put("Number of hours of overtime is ");
    get(overtime);
    --calculate number of hours worked at normal rate
    normal := total_hours − overtime;
    --calculate pay
    basic_pay := normal * rate_of_pay;
    overtime_pay := overtime * overtime_rate;
    pay := basic_pay + overtime_pay;
    put("pay = $");
    put(pay); new_line;
end wages;
```

The symbol "*" is the Ada way of writing a multiplication sign. Six integer variables and two integer constants are declared in this program. The constant identifiers are used to make the program easier to understand.

Execution starts with the prompt

Total number of hours worked is

being output to the user's terminal. Execution of the program is suspended at this point until an integer number such as 38 is typed in at the terminal. This number is read by the program and stored in the variable *total_hours*. A second prompt

Number of hours of overtime is

is then output and execution is again suspended until a second integer number such as 3 is typed in. This is read and stored in the variable *overtime*. The number of normal hours worked and the employee's pay are then calculated and the program prints out the result

    pay = $ 316

Note that if the employee was given a wage rise, all we would have to do is change the constant declarations. The actual program statements would remain unchanged.

3.3 The type integer

In the rest of this chapter we look at the built-in types *integer*, *float*, *character*, *Boolean* and *string*, and at the enumeration types, examining what the values which may be stored in objects of each of these types look like.

The integers are the whole numbers and they may be positive, negative or zero. Integer values or constants can be represented in an Ada program by what are called decimal integer literals. A decimal integer literal consists of a sequence of digits followed optionally by what is called the exponent part. Examples are

37   0   543_210   2e6   2e+6   2000000   2_000_000

The exponent indicates the power of ten by which the preceding integer is to be multiplied to obtain the value. Hence

    2e6   and   2e+6

both represent the value "two times ten to the power six", i.e. two million. A digit sequence may contain isolated underline characters between adjacent digits, but they do not affect the value. They are used to break up long sequences so that they become more readable.

The syntax diagram for a decimal integer literal is

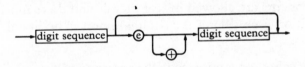

The exponent may be represented by either an upper case "E" or a lower case "e".

We have already seen how integer variables and constants can be declared in object declarations. In chapter 4 we shall look at the arithmetic operations which can be used with integers.

Integers are always represented exactly in a computer, with the minimum and maximum allowed values depending on the implementation. When an integer value is output, sufficient space is allocated to allow for the maximum allowed integer plus a leading space. Numbers with fewer digits are printed with extra leading spaces. Negative integers are preceded by a minus sign.

In our examples we have assumed that the maximum allowed integer has 10 digits. Hence, in Program 3.1, the statements

>   *put*("pay = $"); *put*(*pay*);

printed out

>   pay = $ 316

As this does not always lead to the best way of presenting results, it is possible to have an optional "width parameter". This is shown in the examples

>   *put*('$'); *put*(*pay*, *width* = > 4); -- $ 316 printed
>   *put*('$'); *put*(*pay*, *width* => 3); -- $316 printed

It is not an error for the width parameter to be insufficient to print the whole number; extra space is just taken. In fact, we often use a width parameter of 1 to ensure that the integer will be printed without leading spaces, as in

>   *put*('$'); *put*(*pay*, *width* => 1); -- $316 printed

3.4 The types float and real

Variables of type *float* can be used to store fractional numbers. Fractional numbers are usually referred to as real numbers and they can be represented in Ada programs by what are called decimal real literals. They differ from integer literals in that they have a decimal point. Examples are

>   327.59   297.0   1.0e−6   6.023e23   3.141_592_653

Negative exponents are allowed in real literals and there must be at least one digit on each side of the decimal point. The literal

>   1.0e−6

represents the value "one times ten to the power of minus six", i.e. the number 0.000 001. Underlines are again used to break up long digit sequences to make them more readable.

The syntax diagram for a real literal is

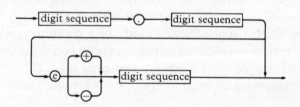

Note that 2 is an integer literal while 2.0 is a real literal. These two numbers will be stored differently in a computer. In general, real numbers are held only approximately and operations with them yield approximate results. This is an important difference from integer operations, where the results are always exact.

The relative precision of the values which can be held in float variables as well as the minimum and maximum possible values depends on which implementation of Ada you are using. As this is far from ideal we are able to specify the relative precision with which fractional numbers are to be stored. We do this by stating the required minimum number of significant decimal digits as follows in what is known as a type declaration.

    type *real* **is digits** 8;

This creates a new floating point type called *real* and values of type *real* are always held to a precision of at least eight decimal digits.

If we have a variable declared as

    sum : *float*;

then the relative accuracy with which the value in *sum* is held depends on which computer you are using. If, on the other hand, we have the declaration

    total : *real*;

then we know that no matter which computer we use the value in *total* will be held with at least eight significant decimal digits.

In this book we assume that the type *real* has been made available through *student_io* and we shall use it when dealing with fractional values.

Example declarations of real variables and constants are

    radius, circumference : *real*;
    frequency, percentage : *real* := 0.0;
    Avogadro : **constant** *real* := 6.023e23;
    pi : **constant** *real* := 3.141_592_7;

The following program again shows how a constant identifier can be used to make a program easier to follow. The program reads in the radius of a circle and calculates its circumference and area.

PROGRAM 3.2

```
with student_io; use student_io;
procedure circle is
   radius, area, circumference : real;
   pi : constant real := 3.141_592_7;
```

```
begin
   --read radius and calculate circumference and area
   put("Radius?");
   get(radius);
   circumference := 2.0 * pi * radius;
   area := pi * radius * radius;
   put("circumference = ");
   put(circumference); new_line;
   put("area = ");
   put(area); new_line;
end circle;
```

Three real variables and one real constant are declared in this program. Execution starts with the prompt

Radius?

being output. The number typed in at the terminal is read and stored in the variable *radius*. The circumference and area of the circle are then calculated using the well-known formulae and the results output with suitable explanatory messages.

3.5 The types character and string

Although much of the publicity about computers gives the impression that they are mostly used for numerical calculations, this is in fact far from being the case. They are used for processing information, and this often involves dealing with strings of characters representing names or text rather than dealing with numbers.

In the programs we have seen so far, strings of characters have been used to write out explanatory messages. We look further at strings below.

Single characters can be stored in variables of type *character*. Character values are represented in Ada programs by character literals, which consist of the character enclosed in apostrophes. Examples are

'a' 'A' '+' ',' ''' ':' ' ' '6'

The space character is represented by a space between two apostrophe characters. It is therefore represented in the same way as any other character.

What are the different characters that may be stored in a character variable, i.e. what is the allowable character set? In Ada, the built-in type *character* allows the 128 characters of what is called the ASCII character set. Of these 128 characters, 95 are printable and the rest are special control characters. Only the 95 printable characters can appear in character literals. The printable characters are the upper and lower case letters, the digits, most commonly used punctuation characters such as comma and semi-colon, and arithmetic operators such as plus and minus. A complete list is given in appendix 3.

The following program gives an example of the use of character variables. It will read in any three characters and write them out again, first together and then separated by spaces.

PROGRAM 3.3

```
with student_io; use student_io;
procedure three_chars is
    char_1, char_2, char_3 : character;
    space : constant character := ' ';
begin
    --read and print three characters
    put("Three characters please:");
    get(char_1); get(char_2); get(char_3);
    --write out the characters
    put(char_1); put(char_2); put(char_3);
    new_line;
    --write again, but include spaces
    put(char_1); put(space);
    put(char_2); put(space); put(char_3);
    new_line;
end three_chars;
```

If the three characters

abc

are typed in as data for this program the result will be

abc

a b c

Characters may be grouped together in a character string, which is a sequence of zero or more characters enclosed by quotation characters. An example is

"This is a string."

String is a built-in type like *integer, float* and *character* but differs from them in one important respect. It is composed of components of a simpler type, namely characters, and so is called a composite type.

The types *integer, float, real* and *character* are examples of what are called scalar types.

Any printable ASCII character may be included in a string. One problem is how to include the quotation character itself without the string being automatically terminated. This problem is solved by using the convention that it has to be written twice. Hence the statement

    put("The variable ""sum"" has been declared.");

will cause the message

    The variable "sum" has been declared.

to be written out.

The empty string is allowed, i.e. a string which contains no characters, and it is written as "".

We have already used strings in our programs. We shall delay the introduction of string variables until later, but deal now with string constants. They are declared as in

    greetings : **constant** *string* := "Hello";

and are useful when a lengthy string is used several times in a program. Consider for example the following program to print out a triangle pattern surrounded by a border:

PROGRAM 3.4

```
with student_io; use student_io;
procedure triangle is
  border : constant string :=
          "*************************";
  spaces : constant string := "          ";
begin
  --print a bordered triangle
  put(border); new_line;
  put(border); new_line;
  new_line;           --produce a blank line
  put(spaces); put(" *"); new_line;
  put(spaces); put(" ***"); new_line;
  put(spaces); put("*****"); new_line;
  new_line;           --another blank line
  put(border); new_line;
  put(border); new_line;
end triangle;
```

The output from this program is

```
*************************
************************
            *
           ***
          *****
*************************
************************
```

In a program a complete string must be written on one line. If this is not possible the catenation operator & can be used. This is best shown by an example. Although the string

"The first part of the string" &
" and the rest of the string"

has been written in two separate parts, it should be regarded as the single string

"The first part of the string and the rest of the string"

3.6 Enumeration types and the type Boolean

In computer programs we frequently have to make logical decisions. Because they are so important, Ada has the built-in type *Boolean* to deal with them. There are only two Boolean values and they are represented in Ada programs by the identifiers *false* and *true*, whose meaning should be self-explanatory. These two identifiers are the Boolean literals.

Example declarations are

flag : *Boolean* := *false*;
success, failure : *Boolean*;
found, finish : *Boolean* := *true*;

The type *Boolean* is an example of what is called an enumeration type.

As has been said several times, it is very important that programs are easy to read and understand. To help us achieve this aim, it is important for us to be able to write programs which deal with problems in as natural a way as possible. If for example a problem involved the days of the week, we could have a convention that the integers 1 to 7 were used to represent the days Sunday to Saturday. It would, however, be much better if we could formulate the solution to our problem by directly using Sunday, Monday, Tuesday, etc.

This is possible in Ada. Up till now we have declared variables and constants, and have used built-in types. It is possible for a programmer to create new types by means of a type declaration. We could for example have a declaration

type *day* **is** (*Sunday, Monday, Tuesday, Wednesday,*
                    Thursday, Friday, Saturday);

which would give us a new type called *day*. This is an example of an enumeration type declaration and *day* is now the name of an enumeration type.

The list of identifiers in brackets gives the possible values which a variable of type *day* may take. These identifiers are called enumeration literals.

Once a new type has been declared, variables and constants of that type can be declared in the normal way. Examples are

weekday : *day* := *Monday*;
arrival : *day*;
midweek : **constant** *day* := *Wednesday*;

As another example of an enumeration type, let us consider the problem of writing a program to play noughts and crosses. At any given point in the game, a square will either be empty or it will contain a nought or a cross. Because the contents of a square can only be one of these three values, a suitable type to introduce into the program would be

type *square* **is** (*nought, cross, empty*);

Variables of type *square* can then be declared and initialised to the value *empty*. An example is

upper_left : *square* := *empty*;

The following syntax diagrams should help us remember the form of an enumeration type declaration:

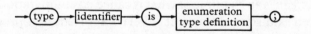

where an enumeration type definition is defined as

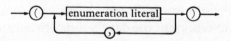

As was said above, the built-in type *Boolean* is an enumeration type. What has happened is that it has been declared behind the scenes as

type *Boolean* **is** (*false*, *true*);

We shall look at expressions involving enumeration literals in chapter 4.

Exercises

1. We have integer literals, real literals, character literals, enumeration literals and character strings. Classify each of the following:

   92   3.5   *false*   4.9e–4   ','   "Sum = "
   4E3   4.0E3   "false"   'a'   3_140_167
   False   ''''   ""''

2. The following values all have different types. What are they?

   9   9.0   '9'   "9"

3. When is it an advantage to use a constant identifier in a program instead of a literal value?

4. Consider the following sequence of Ada declarations:

   sum, total : *integer* := 0;
   type *tree* **is** (*oak, rowan, birch, fir*);
   tall : *tree* := *oak*;
   mountain_ash : **constant** *tree* := *rowan*;
   pressure : *real*;
   letter : *character* := 'a';

   List the variable identifiers and give their type and value. How many of the variables have undefined values?

5. Write declarations for
   (a) the integer variables *number* and *size*,
   (b) a character constant which is aptly called *first_in_alphabet*,
   (c) an enumeration type called *month* which will enable us to deal naturally with the twelve calendar months,
   (d) a variable of type *month*,
   (e) a constant of type *month* which is aptly called *first_month*,
   (f) a string constant whose value is your name.
   (g) a real constant which is aptly called *zero*.

6. Write a program which will request values for the length, breadth and height of a box and will, after reading in these values, calculate and print out the volume of the box.

4

Expressions and assignment

4.1 Introduction

We have already used expressions and assignment statements in our example programs. In Program 3.1 for example, we had the assignment statement

pay := *basic_pay* + *overtime_pay*;

The effect of executing this statement is first to evaluate the expression

basic_pay + *overtime_pay*

and then to assign the resulting value to the variable *pay*.

Expressions are the means by which new values are calculated. The value of the expression

basic_pay + *overtime_pay*

is found by adding the value of the variable *basic_pay* to the value of the variable *overtime_pay*. Expressions consist of one or more of what are called operands, whose values may be combined by operators such as " + " or "*". The operands are usually constant or variable objects. Some example expressions are

94   3 + 2   *first*   2 * *second* + 17   'j'   *pay* > 200

Note that an expression can be an operand on its own.

We have seen that variables and constants have a type as well as a value. In the same way an expression has a type and this depends on its constituent operators and operands. Hence the expression

3 + 2

has the value 5 and is of type *integer*. The expression 'j' is of type *character* and the expression

pay > 200

is of type *Boolean* because it has the value *true* or *false* depending on whether or not the value of the variable *pay* is greater than 200.

In the following sections we shall look in detail at integer, real and Boolean expressions, and at the problem of deciding the order of evaluation in an expression which contains more than one operator.

There is one final general point to be made about expressions. Ada is what is called a strongly typed language. This means that the type of a variable or constant is very important and that values of different types cannot be mixed in expressions. It is not, for example, permissible to add together integer and real values. Similarly in assignment statements the type of the expression on the right of the assignment operator ": = " must be the same as the type of the variable on the left.

4.2 Arithmetic expressions

Arithmetic expressions are concerned with numerical values and the conventional arithmetic operations such as addition, subtraction, multiplication and division. If we assume that a and b are variable identifiers, then the value of the following expressions is found as follows:

$a + b$ the value of the variable a is added to the value of the variable b

$a - b$ the value of the variable b is subtracted from the value of the variable a

$a * b$ the value of the variable a is multiplied by the value of the variable b

a / b the value of the variable a is divided by the value of the variable b

The two variable identifiers a and b must both have been declared to be the same type. If they are integer variables then each of the above expressions is of type *integer*. If they are real variables then each of the expressions is of type *real*.

The effect of integer division is to give an integer value with the remainder being ignored. Hence

     17 / 5   equals 3

Division of two real values gives a real number as a result and so

     17.0 / 5.0   equals 3.4

Ada has a remainder operator **rem**, which is only defined for integer operands. The value of the expression

     a **rem** b

is the value of the remainder after the value of the integer variable a has been divided by the value of the integer variable b. Hence

     17 **rem** 5   equals 2

The operators " + " and " − " normally have two operands, but it is possible for them to have only one. They are then called unary operators. The effect of the operation

   $-a$

is to negate the value of the variable *a*. The unary " + " operator has no effect and so the two expressions

   $+a$ *a*

both have the same value. Another unary operator is **abs**. The value of

   abs *a*

is the absolute value of the variable *a*.

Values can be raised to a power in Ada by the exponentiation operator "**". In the expression

   5**3

the number 3 is called the exponent. It must be an integer. When the exponent is positive the effect of exponentiation is the same as repeated multiplication. Hence 5**3 is equivalent to

   5 * 5 * 5

With integer expressions the exponent must be positive or zero as the result with a negative exponent would not be a whole number. With real expressions the exponent may be a positive or negative integer. Again the effect of exponentiation with a positive exponent is the same as repeated multiplication and so 4.5 ** 3 is equivalent to

   4.5 * 4.5 * 4.5

and the expression 4.5 ** (−3) is equivalent to

   1 / (4.5 * 4.5 * 4.5)

A number raised to the power 0 has the value 1. Hence

   5**0   equals   1
   4.5**0   equals   1.0

When expressions have more than one operator we need rules to indicate the order of evaluation. The rules are the same as in ordinary arithmetic and this gives us, in descending order, the following priority or precedence of the operators:

   1. exponentiation and absolute value;
   2. multiplication, division and remainder;
   3. addition and subtraction.

Where operators have the same precedence, evaluation occurs from left to right, but brackets can be used to change the order of evaluation. The following examples should show what is involved:

9 − 5 + 2	equals 6
9 − (5 + 2)	equals 2
3 + 4 * 5	equals 23
(3 + 4) * 5	equals 35
16 / 2 * 4 * 2	equals 64
16 / (2 * 4 * 2)	equals 1
5 * 2 ** 3	equals 40

4.3 Problem solving

Now that we know how to write assignment statements, let us look at how we can go about solving a simple problem such as how to read a distance in metres and convert it into yards, feet and inches.

As we saw in chapter 1, the first stage in producing a computer program is to construct a suitable outline solution. We call the outline solution the "top-level algorithm". Remember that the kind of algorithm needed to produce a computer program is often exactly the same as the one we would use to solve the problem by ourselves using a pencil and paper. It is therefore useful to think how we would go about solving the problem without a computer. This gives us something like the following solution:

> read the number of metres
> convert metres into inches
> take the number of inches and find the whole number of feet
> and the number of inches left over
> take the number of feet and find the whole number of yards
> and the number of feet left over
> write down the number of yards, feet and inches

The reason for producing a top-level algorithm is to allow us to get the main structure of our solution correct before we become involved in too much detail. This approach to problem solving is called "top-down design".

As this is a very simple problem, we can go directly from this top-level algorithm to its implementation in Ada. Let us first think about the variables which will be required in the program. We are going to require variables to hold the numbers of metres, yards, feet and inches. What is going to be the type of these variables?

It is clear that the number of feet and yards are going to be whole numbers. For the problem to be general, it would seem desirable to allow a real number of metres, but allowing only a whole number of inches would seem suitable although a real number of inches is a possible alternative.

One thing which we have not yet considered is the conversion factor from metres to inches. This is because although it is obviously essential to the solution of the problem, its actual value does not affect the structure of the solution. Once we have got the structure correct we can look up the conversion factor in some textbook.

From what has been said we can see that the following will be required in the program:

> *yards, feet, inches* : *integer*;
> *metres* : *real*;
> *conversion_factor* : **constant** *real* := 39.37;

Let us now consider the implementation of the algorithm. To convert a number of metres to inches we shall multiply the value held in the variable *metres* by the constant *conversion_factor*. This will give us a real value which we shall want to assign to the integer variable *inches*. As we have seen, it is illegal to try to assign the value of a real expression to an integer variable. How, then, do we get round this difficulty?

Ada has special conversion routines which enable us to convert values of one type into corresponding values of another type. To convert an integer object or literal such as 2 into a value of type *real* we write

> *real*(2)

To convert a real object or literal such as 3.7 into an integer value we write

> *integer*(3.7)

When real values are converted into integers they are rounded to the nearest integer. Hence

> *real*(2) + 3.7 gives the value 5.7
> 2 + *integer*(3.7) gives the value 6

The assignment statement to convert a real number of metres into an integer number of inches is

> *inches* := *integer*(*metres* * *conversion_factor*);

Once we have the number of inches, it is straightforward to calculate the equivalent number of yards, feet and inches using the division and remainder operators. The complete program is

PROGRAM 4.1

```
with student_io; use student_io;
procedure convert is
  yards, feet, inches : integer;
  metres : real;
```

```
      conversion_factor : constant real := 39.37;
begin
   --convert metres to yards, feet and inches
   put("number of metres ="); get(metres);
   inches := integer(metres * conversion_factor);
   feet := inches | 12;         -- convert inches to feet
   inches := inches rem 12;     --find number of inches left over
   yards := feet | 3;           -- convert feet to yards
   feet := feet rem 3;          --find number of feet left over
   put(yards); put(" yards");
   put(feet, width = > 2); put(" feet");
   put(inches, width = > 3); put(" inches");
   new_line;
end convert;
```

If the number 2.1 is typed in as data in response to the prompt

   number of metres =

the effects of this program will be to print out the result

   2 yards 0 feet 11 inches

Once you have written a program, it is always a good idea to trace its
execution manually with simple sample data to make sure that it is
doing what you intended. Set the value of *metres* to 2.1 and then
execute the rest of the program for yourself by obeying the assignment
statements in the given order. Once you have done this, check that you
have produced the answer given above.

4.4 Relational expressions

Boolean expressions either have the value *true* or the value
false. A common kind of Boolean expression is the relational expression in which one value is compared with another by means of what is
called a relational operator.

There are six relational operators:

=	equals
/=	not equals
<	less than
< =	less than or equals
>	greater than
> =	greater than or equals

Hence the expression

   3 < 7

gives the value *true* because 3 is less than 7.

There are few restrictions on the kinds of object that can appear in a relational expression. The relational operators can be used to compare integers, reals, characters, strings or the values of any enumeration type, but the usual strict type rules apply and objects may be compared only with other objects of the same type.

The relational operators all have lower precedence than the arithmetic operators. The effect of the expression

$$basic\_pay + overtime\_pay > 200$$

is therefore to add together the value of *basic_pay* and *overtime_pay* and to compare the result with 200. Similarly, assuming that *number* is an integer variable, the expression

$$number \textbf{ rem } 2 = 0$$

is true if the value of *number* is exactly divisible by 2, i.e. if it is even, and is false if it is odd.

When characters are compared the relative order of the character values is given by their order in the ASCII character set given in appendix 3. Most programmers will not be able, and have no need, to remember the relative positions of characters such as ':' and '?', but it is useful to remember that the following relations are all true:

$$'a' < 'b' \quad 'b' < 'c' \quad \ldots \quad 'y' < 'z'$$
$$'A' < 'B' \quad 'B' < 'C' \quad \ldots \quad 'Y' < 'Z'$$
$$'0' < '1' \quad '1' < '2' \quad \ldots \quad '8' < '9'$$

When strings of characters are compared, the value of one string is greater than another string if the value of its first character is greater than the first character of the other string. If both strings have the same first character then the second characters are compared and so on.

The following expressions all have the value *true*:

"Jane" < "Margaret"
"Julie" > "Julia"
"John" > "James"

The empty string is less than any other string and so the expression

"Anne" > "Ann"

is also true.

Being able to compare character strings in this way means that it is possible to write Ada programs to manipulate pieces of text. We can, for example, perform operations such as sorting a list of people's names into alphabetic order. We shall see how to do this in a later chapter.

You will remember from section 3.4 that in a computer real numbers are held only as approximations and that operations with them yield only approximate results. Hence if we have the expression

$$(1.0 \; / \; 3.0) \; \star \; 3.0 \; = \; 1.0$$

we cannot be sure that the result will be true because the expression to the left of the "$=$" operator is likely to evaluate to something like 0.999 999. . . . Equality and inequality operations with real values should therefore be avoided as they often do not give the expected results.

The relative values of the literals of an enumeration type depend on the order in which they were declared. Hence if we have the declaration

> **type** *wedding* **is** (*silver, golden, diamond*);

then the expressions

> *silver* < *golden*
> *golden* < *diamond*

are both true.

4.5 Membership tests

We can determine whether or not a value is within a certain range by using the membership tests **in** and **not in**. For example the expression

> *pay* **in** 150 .. 250

is true if the value of *pay* is within the range 150 to 250 inclusive and is false otherwise. The expression

> *pay* **not in** 150 .. 250

has the opposite effect. The usual strict type rules apply and so *pay* must be of type *integer*.

Using the literals of type *wedding* we find that the expression

> *silver* **in** *golden* .. *diamond*

has the value *false* while

> *silver* **not in** *golden* .. *diamond*

has the value *true*.

Membership tests have the same precedence as the relational operators. If we assume that we have the declarations

> *element, lower* : *integer*;

and that these variables have been given values then the expression *element* **in** *lower* + 3 .. *lower* + 17

is evaluated by first evaluating the expressions *lower* + 3 and *lower* + 17 and then finding if the value of *element* is within this range.

The first value in a range is the lower bound and the second value is the upper bound. If the lower bound is greater than the upper bound then we say that we have a null range. There are no values in a null range.

4.6 Logical operators

It is often useful to link together two or more Boolean expressions. This can be done by means of the logical operators **and, or** and **xor**.

The expression

element **rem** 2 = 0 **and** *element* > 0

is true if the value of *element* is both even and greater than 0; otherwise it is false. The expression

element **rem** 2 = 0 **or** *element* > 0

is true if either of the two relational expressions is true and is false only if they are both false. The expression

element **rem** 2 = 0 **xor** *element* > 15

involves the "exclusive or" operator and is true if one of the two relational expressions is true, but is false if they are both true or both false.

The operators **and, or** and **xor** all have the same precedence, which is lower than that of the relational operators. This is why no brackets are required in the above examples. Extra brackets can be used, however, to help readability as in

(*element* **rem** 2 = 0) **and** *element* > 0

The truth of a Boolean expression can be reversed by means of the unary logical operator **not**. The value of the expression

not (*element* < 4)

is therefore the same as the value of

element > = 4

The **not** operator has higher precedence than multiplication or division.

The following examples should help to show the correct order of evaluation in Boolean expressions, but when in doubt it is a good idea to use extra brackets. In the examples we assume that we have the following declaration:

bright, cheerful : *Boolean*;

The examples are:

not *cheerful* **or** *bright*	--same as (not cheerful) or bright
not (*cheerful* **or** *bright*)	--the brackets have altered the
	--meaning
bright **and not** *cheerful*	--same as bright and (not cheerful)
bright **or** *lower* < 10	--same as bright or (lower < 10)
not (*lower* = 5)	--the brackets are necessary

Brackets must be used in Boolean expressions that contain more than one of the operators **and**, **or** and **xor**. This has the advantage that the order of evaluation is then always clear. The following two expressions have different orders of evaluation and in both cases the brackets are necessary:

(*bright* **and** *cheerful*) **or** *lower* < 10
bright **and** (*cheerful* **or** *lower* < 10)

4.7 Attributes of scalar types

As we have seen, the type of a variable determines the range of values which it may hold and the kind of operations with which it may become involved. Associated with each type are certain attributes such the first, the last, and the relative ordering of its values. With enumeration types this allows their values to be used in relational expressions, with the relative values of the enumeration literals depending on the order in which they were declared.

Hence if we have the declarations

type *day* **is** (*sun, mon, tues, wed, thurs, fri, sat*);
type *card* **is** (*two, three, four, five, six, seven, eight, nine, ten, jack, queen, king, ace*);
appointment : *day* := *wed*;

then the following expressions are true:

appointment = *wed*
mon < *thurs*
four > *two*
jack < *ace*

It is possible to use the attributes of a type directly in an expression. Attributes of a type are written as the type identifier followed first by an apostrophe and then by an identifier specifying the particular attribute. The first and last values of type *day*, for example, are written as

> *day'first*
> *day'last*

and have the values *sun* and *sat* respectively.

Attributes can also be used to find the successor and predecessor of an enumeration value. Examples of these attributes are

> *day'succ(mon)*
> *card'pred(queen)*

which have the values *tues* and *jack*. After execution of the statement

> *appointment* := *day'succ(appointment)*;

the value of *appointment* will have been changed from *wed* to *thurs*. The first value in a type has no predecessor and the last value has no successor.

Attributes are defined not only for enumeration types, but exist for all types in Ada. Some quantities such as the minimum and maximum possible integer or float values vary from one implementation of Ada to the next. You can find out what they are on the system you are using by means of the attributes

> *integer'first   integer'last   float'first   float'last*

If you have to write a program which requires these values it is always good practice to use the attributes rather than the actual values. In this way your program will be less dependent on one particular computer and can more easily be moved to a different machine. On all machines the first integer and float values will be large negative numbers and the last values will be large positive numbers.

The successor and predecessor attributes can be used with integers and characters. The expressions

> *integer'succ(320)*
> *integer'pred(322)*

both give the value 321. However, they are not defined for real values. What, after all, is the successor of 3.156? The *integer, character, Boolean* and other enumeration types whose values have successors and predecessors are called discrete types. All the scalar types we have met except *float* and *real* are discrete.

Other attributes will be introduced at appropriate points in later chapters.

Exercises

1. We have the declarations

   speed : *real* := 35.5;
   time : *real* := 3.0;
   start, stop : *real* := 0.2;
   distance : *real*;

   What will be the values of these variables after the following assignment statements have been executed in the specified order?

   distance := *speed* * *time*;
   time := *start* + *distance* / *speed* + *stop*;
   speed := *distance* / *time*;

2. Assuming the declaration

   centigrade : *integer*;

   what are the values of the expressions

   centigrade * 9 / 5 + 32
   real(*centigrade*) * 1.8 + 32.0

   when *centigrade* has the values 12, 15, 24 and 100.

3. Write a complete Ada program which will read three numbers, calculate their sum and their average, and print the results. Trace the execution of the program when the data is
   2.5   17.3   12.1

4. Evaluate the expressions

   5 + 4 / 3 * 2   17 − 2 + 6   17 − (2 + 6)
   168 / 4 / 2   168 / (4 / 2)   (168 / 4) / 2
   30 * 4 / 5   30 * (4 / 5)
   2 + 3 < 6 **and** 15 <= 12   "Mary" > "Margaret"
   card'succ(*card'first*)   *integer'first* < 0
   six **not in** *ten* .. *card'last*

5. Assume that you have two integer variables *first* and *second* which have been assigned values. Write Boolean expressions for each of the following situations:

   (*a*) *first* is greater than *second*
   (*b*) *first* is exactly divisible by *second*
   (*c*) both *first* and *second* are greater than or equal to zero
   (*d*) either *first* or *second* is greater than zero but not both
   (*e*) *first* is greater than or equal to 1 and is less than or equal to 6

6. We have the declarations

   type *day* **is** (*sun, mon, tues, wed, thurs, fri, sat*);
   my_appointment : *day* := *mon*;
   your_appointment : *day* := *wed*;
   intermediate : *day*;

   What are the values of the variables after evaluation of each of
   the following sets of assignment statements?

   (*a*) *intermediate* := *my_appointment*;
       my_appointment := *your_appointment*;
       your_appointment := *intermediate*;

   (*b*) *my_appointment* := *your_appointment*;
       your_appointment := *my_appointment*;

7. If the annual inflation rate is x % then after n years \$1000 will
   be worth

   \$1000 * (100 / (100 + x)) ** n

   Write a program which will read values for x and n, and then
   calculate how much \$1000 is worth after n years.

5

Selection and repetition

5.1 Selection

In the program which we developed in chapter 4 the same statements are executed in exactly the same order each time the program is run. If all programs were like this we would not have a very powerful or flexible tool. What we need is to be able to select which statement is to be executed next, with the decision depending on what has happened so far.

In Ada the statement which allows us to do this is the if statement. It uses a Boolean expression to select the appropriate path.

To see how this is done let us look again at Program 4.1, where we converted a number of metres into the equivalent number of yards, feet and inches. The results were printed out using the statements

put(yards); *put*(" yards");
put(feet, width = > 2); *put*(" feet");
put(inches, width = > 3); *put*(" inches");

In the sample run the result

2 yards 0 feet 11 inches

was printed out, but it might be thought that a better way of presenting the results would be to print the number of yards or feet only when they are non-zero.

This can be achieved using the following statements:

if *yards* > 0 **then**
    put(yards); *put*(" yards");
end if;
if *feet* > 0 **then**
    put(feet, width = > 2); *put*(" feet");
end if;
put(inches, width = > 3); *put*(" inches");

Here we have two examples of the if statement. Using our sample data, execution occurs as follows. We first evaluate the Boolean expression which follows the reserved word **if**. Because the number of yards is 2, the value of *yards* > 0 is *true* and the statements between the reserved words **then** and **end if**

   put(*yards*); *put*(" yards");

are executed.

We now proceed to the next statement, which is another if statement. The Boolean expression *feet* > 0 is evaluated and because it is false the two statements between **then** and **end if**

   put(*feet*, *width* = > 2); *put*(" feet");

are skipped. Finally the statements

   put(*inches*, *width* = > 3); *put*(" inches");

are executed. Thus there is always some output even in the case where we have zero metres. The net effect is to print

   2 yards 11 inches

This has been our first example of a compound statement. Although the if statement contains other statements, it is considered to be a single statement.

The solution to a problem often involves the choice between alternative courses of action or, indeed, choosing one out of several different possible courses. Other versions of the if statement allow us to deal with such cases. If for example *a* has been declared to be of type *integer*, the if statement

   if *a* > 0 **then**
      put("greater than zero");
   else
      put("not greater than zero");
   end if;

is executed by evaluating the expression *a* > 0 and then either obeying the statement after **then** or the statement after the reserved word **else**, depending on whether or not the relational expression is true.

In the statement

   if *a* > 0 **then**
      put("greater than zero");
   elsif *a* < 0 **then**
      put("less than zero");
   else
      put("equal to zero");
   end if;

we first evaluate the expression *a* > 0 and if it is true the statement following **then** is obeyed. Only if it is false do we go on to evaluate the expression $a < 0$ following the reserved word **elsif**. If it is true then the statement following the second **then** is executed, but if that is also false then the statement following **else** is executed.

Let us now look at the general form of the if statement. In the syntax diagram a "sequence of statements" is defined to be one or more statements.

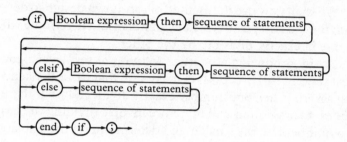

In the execution of an if statement, we start by evaluating the Boolean expression following **if**. If it is true the sequence of statements following **then** is executed. Only when it is false do we proceed to the rest of the statement, where there may be zero or more "elsif parts". The Boolean expressions following any occurrences of **elsif** are evaluated in turn until one is true. The corresponding sequence of statements is then executed. If none of the Boolean expressions are true then, if there is an optional "else part", the sequence of statements following **else** is executed.

The following example shows an if statement with more than one **elsif**. The variable *ch* is assumed to have been declared to be of type *character*.

```
if ch in 'a' .. 'z' then
    put("lower case");
elsif ch in 'A' .. 'Z' then
    put("upper case");
elsif ch in '0' .. '9' then
    put("digit");
else
    put("other character");
end if;
```

The membership expressions are evaluated in turn until one is true. The appropriate message is then printed. If they are all false

other characters

is printed.

Note that in the layout of the example statements, the reserved words **if, elsif, else** and **end** are written under one another and the statements in the enclosed sequences of statements are indented. This is to make the structure of the statement clear to a human reader.

5.2 **Program development**

We shall now use the method of top-down design to develop a program to read two positive whole numbers and determine whether or not one is exactly divisible by the other.

We start by producing an outline solution or top-level algorithm. The first stage in this process is to make sure that we understand what is being asked. When one number exactly divides another there is no remainder. Our solution will therefore involve dividing the larger of the two numbers by the smaller and determining if the remainder is zero.

This leads to the problem of not knowing which number is the larger, but this can be overcome by swapping them around if necessary to ensure, for example, that the first is always greater than or equal to the second. This approach gives the following outline solution:

> read two numbers
> if the second is greater than the first then
> swap first and second
> end if
> find remainder when the first is divided by the second
> if remainder is 0 then
> write that one is divisible by the other
> else
> write that one is not divisible by the other
> end if

The algorithm has been written in a restricted form of English which can be regarded as an informal "program design language". This allows us to reason about the design of our solution before we become involved with implementing it in Ada. An algorithm usually involves sequencing, selection and repetition. The sequence in which the statements have to be obeyed is given by the order in which they are written. Selection can be specified by the stilted English construction

> if condition is true then
> do something
> else

```
    do something else
  end if
```

Repetition is dealt with in the next section. Indentation is used, as in programs, to show the structure of the proposed solution.

Each statement in a top-level algorithm can be thought of as the specification of some subproblem which has still to be solved. When we write a top-level algorithm we are therefore splitting our initial problem into several fairly independent subproblems, each of which should be easier to solve than the original. This is the basic principle of top-down design. It allows us to concentrate on the structure of the solution as a whole without having to worry about how each sub-problem is going to be solved. Detailed consideration of the subproblems is postponed to a later stage. We have, for example, shelved consideration of the problem of how to swap two values.

Our aim is therefore to get the overall structure of our solution correct before we get bogged down in too much detail.

In our simple example it is straightforward to implement the solution to most of the subproblems directly in Ada, but in general some of the subproblems may have to be split into a series of yet smaller problems. We go about producing the solution to a subproblem in the same way as we produced the solution to the original problem.

This approach to problem solving has been given several different names, the most common of which are top-down design, structured programming and programming by stepwise refinement.

Once we have an outline solution we should test that it works correctly by manually tracing its execution with sample data. This should be done with several different sets of data carefully chosen so that each part of the algorithm is tested by at least one of the sets.

We should also have another look at our strategy to see if we have overlooked any problems. You will find that it is often easier to spot and deal with problems before they become hidden by detail. In this example there is a problem. If a number is divided by zero the answer is infinity and so our solution must be modified to guard against this possibility.

Producing a solution is not therefore a simple linear process, but an iterative one where earlier decisions have to be changed in the light of fuller information. The outline algorithm now becomes

```
    read two numbers
    if the second is greater than the first then
      swap first and second
    end if
```

```
if the second is 0 then
  write suitable message
else
  find remainder when the first is divided by the second
  if remainder is 0 then
    write that one is divisible by the other
  else
    write that one is not divisible by the other
  end if
end if
```

Once this version of the algorithm has been tested we can consider the problem of swapping two values. This is straightforward as long as we remember that an intermediate variable is required.

```
remember the original value of the first number
set the first to the value of the second
set the second number to the original value of the first
```

As the main structure of our solution has now been developed, we are in a position to implement it in Ada. The program is:

PROGRAM 5.1

```
with student_io; use student_io;
procedure divisible is
  first, second : integer; --the input data
  intermediate : integer; --used in swapping
  remainder : integer;
begin
  --find if one number can exactly divide another
  put("two positive integers please ");
  get(first); get(second);
  --ensure that first > = second
  if second > first then
    intermediate := first;
    first := second;
    second := intermediate;
  end if;
  if second = 0 then
    put("Cannot divide by zero");
  else
    --calculate remainder
    remainder := first rem second;
    if remainder = 0 then
      put(first, width = > 1);
```

```
            put(" is exactly divisible by ");
            put(second, width = > 1);
      else
            put("Not exactly divisible");
      end if;
   end if;
      new_line;
   end divisible;
```

You should trace the execution of this program with sample data to convince yourself that it is correct. Remember to trace the program with different sets of data chosen so that each part of the program is tested at least once. The conditions to be tested in this example are

  (i) first greater than or equal to second,
 (ii) first less than second,
(iii) exactly divisible,
(iv) not exactly divisible,
 (v) attempt to divide by zero.

Suitable pairs of input numbers are

  21   7
   9 18
  10 18
   6   0

with each pair testing more than one of the conditions.

Note that in the program one of the if statements is nested within another if statement. This causes no problem because it is quite clear where each one begins and ends. In Ada there is no restriction on the kind of statement which can appear within an inner sequence of statements.

5.3 Short circuit logical operations

In our last example we found that before we attempted a division it was necessary for us to check that we were not trying to divide by zero. Would it have been possible to simplify the program by incorporating both this check and the test of whether or not we had a remainder into a single Boolean expression?

What we want to be able to do is to check that the divisor is non-zero and to perform the remainder operation only when this condition is true. This might lead us to try the expression

$$second \; |= 0 \; \textbf{and} \; (first \; \textbf{rem} \; second = 0)$$

After all, if *second* $|= 0$ is false then the whole Boolean expression must be false. This is not a solution however, as both operands of an **and** operator are always evaluated and the order in which this is done is not specified. Evaluation of this expression could therefore involve division by zero.

To deal with cases like this where we want to check one condition and then check a second condition only if it can affect the result, Ada has short circuit evaluation. In the expression

second /= 0 **and then** (*first* **rem** *second* = 0)

the condition *second* /= 0 is first evaluated and only if it is true is the other condition tested. This gives the desired protection against division by zero.

As well as **and then** we also have **or else**. In the condition

second = 0 **or else** (*first* **rem** *second* /= 0)

the whole Boolean expression must be true if *second* is equal to zero and so the relational expression after **or else** is evaluated only when *second* is non-zero.

The short circuit operations are designed for situations in which the order of evaluation is important. Normally, as in the above example, this is the case when there are circumstances in which we wish to inhibit evaluation of the second condition.

Let us now rewrite our program to determine whether one number is exactly divisible by another.

PROGRAM 5.2

```
with student_io; use student_io;
procedure divisible is
   first, second : integer; -- the input data
   intermediate : integer; --used in swapping
begin
   --find if one number can exactly divide another
   put("two positive integers please ");
   get(first); get(second);
   --ensure that first > = second
   if second > first then
      intermediate := first;
      first := second;
      second := intermediate;
   end if;
   if second /= 0 and then (first rem second = 0) then
      put(first, width = > 1);
      put(" is exactly divisible by ");
      put(second, width = > 1);
```

```
    else
        put("Not exactly divisible");
    end if;
    new_line;
end divisible;
```

5.4 Repetition

Computers are ideally suited to the solution of problems which involve repeating the same or similar operations a very large number of times.

Let us consider the following problem. We have a list of one or more positive numbers followed by a negative number, and we want to read the positive numbers one by one and find their sum.

This is a straightforward problem to solve without a computer. We take each number in turn and add it to the sum so far, i.e. we repeatedly perform the operations

> read a number
> add the number to the sum

When we come across the negative number we know that we have come to the end of our list and can stop. This approach forms the basis of our computer solution.

In Ada a loop statement is used when we wish to execute the same sequence of statements repeatedly. Each time round the loop we perform a test to see whether we should continue or leave the loop. This can be done by an exit statement which, as we might expect, uses a Boolean expression to make the decision.

Assuming the declarations

> *sum, number* : *real*;

the following Ada statements will solve our problem:

```
sum := 0.0; --the sum is initially set to zero
loop
    get(number);
    exit when number < 0.0;
    sum := sum + number;
    --sum contains the total so far
end loop;
```

The value of *sum* is set to zero and we then enter the loop. A number is read and then tested in the exit statement to see if it is less than zero. If it is we leave the loop and execute the statement following **end loop**. Otherwise we continue on to the next statement, where the

number is added to the current value of the sum. The reserved words
end loop are then encountered and we return to the beginning of the
loop, where the next number is read and tested. We continue round
the loop in this way until the exit statement is executed with a negative
number.

Hence if the data read was

14.6 15.3 75.2 9.7 67.3 -1.2

we would sum the first five numbers and leave the loop after reading
and testing the sixth number.

It is possible to write a program in which the exit condition never
becomes true. This results in what is called an "infinite loop" and is
an error normally caused by faulty logic in the development of the
program.

The general form of a basic loop is

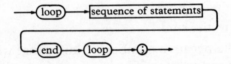

and an exit statement has the form

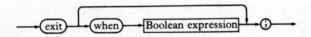

There are two forms of the exit statement, the conditional and the
unconditional exit. The following example shows how they are related. The meaning of the statement

exit when *number* < 0.0;

is exactly the same as

if *number* < 0.0 **then**
  exit;
end if;

but the former is to be preferred. It is important that programs are
easy to read and understand, and significant events, such as where the
loop may be left, should be as prominent as possible. Otherwise,
because a loop may contain more than one exit statement, one could be
overlooked.

The following program uses a loop to read in a sentence and
calculate how many upper case letters, lower case letters, blanks and

punctuation or other characters it contains. The sentence may extend over more than one line.

PROGRAM 5.3

```
with student_io; use student_io;
procedure sentence is
   capital_count, lower_count, blank_count,
      punct_count : integer := 0; --counts initialised
   ch : character;
begin
   --Program to read and analyse the characters in a sentence
   put("Type in a sentence please ");
   loop
      --get and classify the next character
      get(ch);
      if ch in 'a' .. 'z' then
         lower_count := lower_count + 1;
      elsif ch in 'A' .. 'Z' then
         capital_count := capital_count + 1;
      elsif ch = ' ' then
         blank_count := blank_count + 1;
      else
         punct_count := punct_count + 1;
      end if;
      --the counts contain the totals so far
      exit when ch = '.';
   end loop;
   put("The number of capitals is ");
   put(capital_count, width => 1); new_line;
   put("The number of lower case letters is ");
   put(lower_count, width => 1); new_line;
   put("The number of blanks is ");
   put(blank_count, width => 1); new_line;
   put("The number of punctuation characters is ");
   put(punct_count, width => 1); new_line;
end sentence;
```

If the sentence typed in as data is

It is a long, long way
to Tipperary.

the following results will be obtained by running the program:

The number of capitals is 2
The number of lower case letters is 25
The number of blanks is 6
The number of punctuation characters is 2

The different counts are initialised to zero during their declaration. Each time round the loop the next character is read and one of the four counts is incremented. We then test for the end of the sentence, i.e. for a full stop. When a full stop is encountered we leave the loop; otherwise we return to the beginning of the loop where the next character is read. Note that the final full stop is part of the sentence and is counted as a punctuation character.

5.5 Loop invariants

Once you have written several programs you will find that when presented with a new problem we do not have to start from scratch but can make use of our experience. This is essential if we are ever to solve large problems. Quite a few problems, although they might appear to be distinct, have solutions which are essentially the same. As an example of this we may again consider the list of one or more positive numbers terminated by a negative number, but this time we wish to find which number is the largest.

Let us see if we can use our experience to help solve this problem. When we found the sum of the numbers we used a loop and each time round the loop we calculated the "sum so far". When we analysed the sentence we used a loop and each time round we updated the "counts so far". The solution to our problem might therefore be to use a loop and each time round calculate the "largest number so far".

The following sequence of statements uses this strategy to solve the problem. The declarations

   number, largest : real;

are assumed.

```
get(largest);
--largest contains the largest value so far
loop
  get(number);
  exit when number < 0.0;
  --if necessary update largest
  if number > largest then
    largest := number;
  end if;
  --largest contains the largest value so far
end loop;
--largest contains the largest value
```

As there is no competition, the first number read must be the largest so far. Each time round the loop we read the next number, exit if the number is less than zero and otherwise update, when necessary, the value of *largest*.

The comment

--largest contains the largest value so far

is an assertion which is true before the loop starts and remains true after each iteration. We call this assertion the "loop invariant". When designing a loop as part of the solution to a problem it is of great help to identify the loop invariant so that we know what we have to achieve each time round the loop.

If the final program contains a statement of the loop invariant as a comment this can greatly help our understanding of what the program is trying to achieve.

5.6 **The while loop**

It is common for a loop to have only one exit and for that exit to be at the beginning. To deal with this case we have a special form of the loop statement called the while loop

The following example shows how it is used. We want to be able to find the sum of the odd numbers between 1 and some limit, which has been read as data. If the declarations

limit : *integer*;
odd_number : *integer* := 1;
sum_odd : *integer* := 0;

are assumed, the statements to solve this problem are

get(*limit*);
while *odd_number* < = *limit* **loop**
  sum_odd := *sum_odd* + *odd_number*;
  odd_number := *odd_number* + 2;
  --sum_odd contains the sum of the odd numbers so far
end loop;

After the value of the limit has been read, we start the loop. The Boolean expression followed the reserved word **while** is evaluated and, if it is true, the sequence of statements between **loop** and **end loop** are executed. We then return to the beginning of the loop where the Boolean expression is again evaluated. If it is still true we again execute the statements in the loop. We continue round the loop in this way "while the Boolean expression is true".

In our example the value of the odd number increases each time round the loop and will eventually exceed the limit. Once this has happened, the next time the Boolean expression is evaluated it will be false and so the loop will be terminated.

A while loop can always be rewritten in terms of a basic loop and an exit statement. The effect of the above loop, for example, is exactly the same as

```
get(limit);
loop
   exit when odd_number > limit;
   sum_odd := sum_odd + odd_number;
   odd_number := odd_number + 2;
   --sum_odd contains the sum of the odd numbers so far
end loop;
```

Note that if the value read in for the limit is less than one then the statements within the loop are not executed at all.

A while loop can contain an exit statement, but this is not advisable. The reason for there being a special while loop is to help program readability and reliability. If a loop starts with

```
while odd_number <= limit loop
```

we are, in a way, making a promise that we are going to go round the loop while evaluation of this condition gives the value *true*. If an exit statement is included within the loop, this promise will be broken because there will then be an alternative way of leaving the loop. This is very likely to mislead someone reading the program or, indeed, to mislead the person who wrote the program when he or she comes to read it some time later.

If it is felt that the use of an exit statement is the best way of solving a particular problem then the fact that the loop can be left in more than one way should be advertised in a comment at the beginning of the loop.

5.7   **The for loop**

In the example where we read and analysed the characters in a sentence we did not know, when the loop was started, how often it was to be executed. We stopped after a full stop had been read, but there was no way of foretelling when that would be. The while loop and the basic loop plus exit statement are designed to deal with the many problems of this nature.

Ada has a special form of loop to deal with cases where we go round a loop a known number of times. Its use is best seen by means of a simple example.

Assuming the declaration

sum : integer := 0;

the following loop will sum the numbers from 1 to 100:

for *count* **in** 1 .. 100 **loop**
   sum := sum + count;
end loop;

The identifier *count* is called the "loop parameter". The statement between **loop** and **end loop** is executed 100 times, with the loop parameter taking in turn each of the values in the range 1 to 100.

We do not have to declare the loop parameter because it is implicitly declared when it appears in the for loop and its type is determined by the type of the range expression. The first time round the loop it has the value of the lower bound of the range and is then automatically incremented before each subsequent cycle round the loop. It is illegal to try to change the value of a loop parameter within a loop by an assignment statement or by any other means.

Let us now look at a more complicated example. We have information about a class of students. Each student has taken three exams. To be given a merit pass a student must achieve more than 60% in each exam. To be given an ordinary pass a student must achieve an average of more than 50%. The data is ordered so that the first three exam results refer to the first student, the next three to the next student and so on. At the beginning of the list of data we are given the class size. Our problem is to find how many students have gained a merit pass, how many an ordinary pass and how many have failed.

The first stage in producing a solution is to make sure that we understand exactly what is being asked. Then, as we have done in our earlier examples, we think how we should set about solving the problem, without paying too much attention to the fact that we are going to use a computer. This should lead us to the following outline solution:

    initialise counts
    read size of class
    loop for each person in the class
        deal with this student's exam results
        update the count for the relevant student category
    end loop
    write results

Most of the statements in this algorithm can easily be implemented in Ada. It is really only the statement

deal with this student's exam results

which requires further expansion. Having settled on the main structure, we are now in a position to concentrate on this subproblem knowing that when it has been solved we shall have produced a solution which will deal with all the students' exam results.

There is normally more than one way of solving a problem and it is not always obvious which is best. In this case the following method of dealing with each student's results works satisfactorily:

read the three exam results
determine if a merit pass, an ordinary pass or a fail

This approach requires that the three exam results be read and stored before we do any processing. If instead of three we had a large number of results per student, this would have drawbacks.

An alternative approach is to deal with each exam result as it is read in:

initialise exam total and set merit marker to true
loop three times
   read an exam result
   set merit marker to false if the exam result < = 60
   add exam result to the total so far
end loop
calculate average mark

This second approach can easily be modified to deal with any number of exams per student. As it is more interesting, it has been used in the production of the final program.

PROGRAM 5.4

```
with student_io; use student_io;
procedure statistics is
    exam_result, class_size, exam_total : integer;
    merit_flag : Boolean;
    merit_passes, ord_passes, fails : integer := 0;
    no_of_exams : constant integer := 3;
begin
    --gather statistics on students' performance
    put("Number in class?");
    get(class_size);
    for student in 1 .. class_size loop
        --deal with the next student's exam results
        merit_flag := true;
```

```
exam_total := 0;
for exam in 1 .. no_of_exams loop
  get(exam_result);
  if exam_result < = 60 then
    merit_flag := false;
  end if;
  exam_total := exam_total + exam_result;
end loop;
--if merit flag still true all results > 60
if merit_flag then
  merit_passes := merit_passes + 1;
elsif exam_total / no_of_exams > 50 then
  ord_passes := ord_passes + 1;
else
  fails := fails + 1;
end if;
--the counts give information on the students so far
end loop;
put("Number of merit passes = ");
put(merit_passes, width = > 1); new_line;
put("Number of ordinary passes = ");
put(ord_passes, width = > 1); new_line;
put("number of fails = ");
put(fails, width = > 1); new_line;
end statistics;
```

If there are 25 students in the class we shall go round the outer loop 25 times. Each time round we come across the inner loop

for *exam* **in** 1 .. *no_of_exams* **loop**

The statements within this inner loop are executed three times before we continue on to the statements where the relevant count is updated. The program therefore reads and processes 25 * 3 = 75 exam results.

There is a form of the for loop in which the loop parameter takes the values in the range in reverse order. For example, the statement

for *ch* **in reverse** 'a' .. 'z' **loop**
　　put(ch);
end loop;

will print the alphabet in reverse order.

The general form of the for loop can be shown by a syntax diagram:

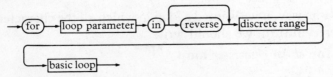

We must use a discrete range in a for loop because only the values of discrete types have successors and predecessors. A loop parameter cannot therefore be of type *real*.

The lower and upper bounds in the discrete range are expressions which are evaluated once, before the loop is started. If, assuming the relevant declarations, we have

for *student* **in** *base* + *offset* .. *size* * 2 **loop**

the values of the expressions *base* + *offset* and *size* * 2 are evaluated before the loop is entered. If any of these variables are changed during execution of the loop this will have no effect on the number of loop iterations. If the lower bound is initially greater than the upper bound, the statements within the loop are not executed at all.

As you would expect, variables of an enumeration type can be used to control a for loop. Given the declarations

```
type month is (jan, feb, march, april, may, june, july, aug, sep,
               oct, nov, dec);
no_of_visitors : integer;
income : integer := 0;
summer_price : constant integer := 3;
other_price : constant integer := 2;
```

we can calculate the annual income from the sale of visitors' tickets at an ancient monument. The admission charges are higher in the summer months.

```
for this_month in jan .. dec loop
    get(no_of_visitors);
    if this_month in june .. sep then
        income := income + no_of_visitors * summer_price;
    else
        income := income + no_of_visitors * other_price;
    end if;
end loop;
```

To emphasise that in the loop we are going from the first to the last possible value in the enumeration type we could have written

for *this_month* **in** *month'first* .. *month'last* **loop**

As a further alternative we could have just written the type name, as in

for *this_month* **in** *month* **loop**

In the same way, if we wanted a loop in which all the characters were considered in turn, we should write

for *ch* **in** *character* **loop**

We can have exit statements within a for loop but, as with their use in while loops, this is not advisable because it tends to obscure the basic structure of a program and may therefore make it harder to read and understand.

5.8 The case statement

We have seen how an if statement can be used to select which sequence of statements should be executed next. When there is a large number of possible alternatives a case statement is often easier to understand.

The example in which the annual income from the sale of tickets was calculated can be re-written as

```
for this_month in month loop
    get(no_of_visitors);
    case this_month is
        when june .. sep = >
            income := income + no_of_visitors * summer_price;
        when jan .. may | oct .. dec = >
            income := income + no_of_visitors * other_price;
    end case;
end loop;
```

The expression between the reserved words **case** and **is** is evaluated and this determines which of the sequences of statements is to be executed. Each of the alternatives is labelled with a list of one or more choices. The choices must be constant expressions or constant discrete ranges and they are separated by the symbol "|", which should be read as "or". Naturally the usual strict type rules apply and the choices must have the same type as the expression following **case**. This must be a discrete type.

The next example assumes the declarations

```
leap_year : Boolean;
which_month : month;
no_of_days : integer;
```

and that these variables have been given suitable values. The appropriate number of days in a month can be calculated as follows:

```
case which_month is
    when april | june | sep | nov = >
        no_of_days := 30;
    when feb = >
        if leap_year then
```

```
          no_of_days := 29;
      else
          no_of_days := 28;
      end if;
   when jan | march | may | july | aug | oct | dec =>
      no_of_days := 31;
end case;
```

Each possible value which can be taken by the expression after **case** must correspond to one, and only one, of the choices. In our example there are 12 values in type *month* and they are all catered for in the case statement. To deal with types which have a large range of values the reserved word **others** can be used to specify all alternatives which have not been given explicitly. The **others** alternative must always be the last of the alternative sequences.

Although the above example could be re-written with the final alternative labelled with **others**, as in

when others =>
   no_of_days := 31;

the first version is to be preferred because it is then much clearer which months have 31 days.

The syntax of the case statement is best summarised by its syntax diagram,

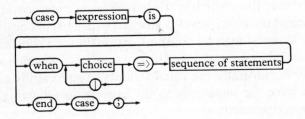

with choice being defined by

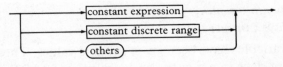

Exercises

1. Trace the execution of the following Ada program when it is presented with the data

   21, 7, 28, 14;

```
with student_io; use student_io;
procedure large is
   largest, number : integer;
   char : character;
begin
   get(largest); get(char);
   while char /= ';' loop
      get(number); get(char);
      if number > largest then
         largest := number;
      end if;
   end loop;
   put("The largest number is ");
   put(largest); new_line;
end large;
```

2. We saw in section 5.1 how an if statement could be used to determine whether a character was a capital letter, a lower case letter, a digit or some other character. Rewrite the if statement as a case statement.

3. What would be the effect of executing the following statements, where *ch* has been declared to be of type *character*?

```
ch := 'a';
while ch <= 'z' loop
   put(ch);
   ch := character'succ(ch);
end loop;
```

What for loop would have the same effect?

4. In Ada we can use a basic loop with one or more exit statements, a while loop or a for loop. Under which circumstances is each of these different kinds of loop to be preferred over the others?

5. After first designing suitable outline solutions, write Ada programs which will

   (i)   read three numbers and find the smallest
   (ii) read one hundred numbers and find the smallest
   (iii) read a whole number n and then calculate
         $$1 + 1/2 + 1/3 + \ldots + 1/n$$
   (iv) read a whole number n and then calculate
         $$1 - 1/2 + 1/3 \ldots 1/n$$

6. You have $500 in your bank account and each week your income is $100 and your expenditure is $110. At the end of each 12-week period, interest of 2.5 % of your current balance is added to your account. Write a program to calculate how long it will be before you run out of money.

7. Re-write the program in question 6 so that it will be able to cope with any value of initial sum, weekly income, weekly expenditure and rate of interest.

8. What would be the effect of executing the following program?

```
with student_io; use student_io;
procedure mowing is
begin
    for verses in 2 .. 10 loop
      put(verses, width = > 2);
      put(" men went to mow, went to mow a meadow,");
      new_line;
      for men in reserve 2 .. verses loop
        put(men, width = > 2);
        put(" men"); new_line;
      end loop;
      put(" 1 man and his dog, went to mow a meadow.");
      new_line; new_line;
    end loop;
end mowing;
```

6

Input and output

6.1 Presentation of results

Our example programs have assumed that data is typed in at the keyboard of an interactive terminal and that results are either displayed on the terminal's VDU screen or printed at the terminal. The use of an interactive terminal allows a user to interact with the running of a program, and we have seen how prompts, messages and results can be output and how data can be read in.

It is important that the results of a program are presented in such a way that they are easy to read and understand. To do this we need to have control over their layout. The *width* parameter allows us to do this with integer values. If we have the declaration

number : *integer* := 17;

the effect of executing

put("value ="); *put*(*number, width* => 1); *new_line*;
put("value ="); *put*(*number, width* => 2); *new_line*;
put("value ="); *put*(*number, width* => 4); *new_line*;

is to print out

value = 17
value = 17
value =   17

When a larger value than is absolutely necessary is specified for the width, an appropriate number of spaces is output in front of the number. It is not an error when too small a width is specified; the required amount of space is just used. If a width is not specified, sufficient space is allocated to allow the value of *integer'last* to be output, preceded by a space. This value differs from one implementation of Ada to the next and you should find out what it is on the system you are using.

The statement

   put(number, 2);

has the same effect as

   put(number, width = > 2);

and has the advantage of brevity. The longer form is recommended however, for the meaning of the statement is then much clearer.

The output of real values is more complicated. They are normally printed in what is called "floating point form". Let us look at this with an example. If we have the declaration

   amount : real := 12345.678;

then the statements

   put("number = "*); put(amount);*

will print out

   number = 1.2345678E + 04

Positive real values are preceded by a space and negative values by a minus sign. There is then a single non-zero digit before the decimal point, except in the case where 0.0 is being output. The number of places after the decimal point is one less than the number of significant digits given in the definition of type *real*. Finally we have the exponent part, which is always output with an initial plus or minus sign followed by two digits. The value printed above should be read as "1.2345678 times 10 to the power 4".

Just as it was possible to control the spacing of integer values, we can also control the layout of real values. The number of print positions before the decimal point is controlled by the *fore* parameter, the number of digits printed after the decimal point by the *aft* parameter and the number of print positions used in the exponent by the *exp* parameter. Hence

   put("number = "*); put(amount, fore = >* 3*); new_line;*
   put("number = "*); put(amount, aft = >* 5*); new_line;*
   put("number = "*); put(amount, fore = >* 1, *aft = >* 3,
      exp = > 2*); new_line;*
   put("number = "*); put(amount,* 1, 3, 2*); new_line;*

will print out

   number =   1.2345678E + 04
   number = 1.23457E + 04
   number = 1.235E + 4
   number = 1.235E + 4

If we want to print real values without an exponent part we set the *exp* parameter to zero. Execution of the statements

> *put*("number = "); *put*(*amount, aft* = > 2, *exp* = > 0);
> *new_line*;
> *put*("number = "); *put*(*amount, fore* = > 8, *aft* = > 1,
>   *exp* = > 0);

will print

> number = 12345.68
> number =   12345.7

If no value is given for *fore*, sufficient space is taken before the decimal point to allow the number to be printed. Negative numbers are printed with a leading minus sign and positive numbers with a leading space.

When *put* is used to output character or string values there is no optional parameter like *width* to output a variable number of leading blanks. However, because we often want a new line to be taken after a string value has been printed, we can write

> *put_line*("Hello");

which has the same effect as

> *put*("Hello"); *new_line*;

One of the situations where it is important to have close control over layout is when we wish to display our results as a table. As an example, the following program shows how the values of the circumference, volume and the surface area of a sphere change as the radius increases:

PROGRAM 6.1

```
with student_io; use student_io;
procedure tabulate is
    pi : constant real := 3.141_59;
    rr : real;
begin
    --tabulate properties of sphere as radius changes
    put_line("radius   circumference   volume   surface");
    put_line("                                  of sphere");
    for r in 1 .. 10 loop
        put(r, width = > 6);
        rr := real(r);
        --write circumference
        put(2.0 * pi * rr, fore = > 5, aft = > 3, exp = > 0);
        --write volume
```

```
        put(4.0 / 3.0 * pi * rr ** 3, fore => 11, aft => 3);
        --write surface area
        put(4.0 * pi * rr * rr, fore => 6, aft => 3);
        new_line;
    end loop;
  end tabulate;
```

Running this program will produce the following results:

radius	circumference	volume	surface of sphere
1	6.283	4.189E+00	1.257E+01
2	12.566	3.351E+01	5.027E+01
3	18.850	1.131E+02	1.131E+02
4	25.133	2.681E+02	2.011E+02
5	31.416	5.236E+02	3.142E+02
6	37.699	9.048E+02	4.524E+02
7	43.982	1.437E+03	6.158E+02
8	50.265	2.145E+03	8.042E+02
9	56.549	3.054E+03	1.018E+03
10	62.832	4.189E+03	1.257E+03

It is very easy to make a mistake in working out the required spacing for the table headings and, because the *fore* parameter is being used to control the spacing between the numbers, further mistakes are likely there. Easier control of the layout can be achieved if we consider a line of output to be a series of columns with one character printed per column. At each stage in the output we have a current column number whose value is updated after each *put* statement. This current column number can also be set by a *set_col* statement. Assuming that *position* is of type *integer*, the effect of the statement

    set_col(position);

depends on the value of *position*. If it is greater than the current column number then sufficient blanks are output to set the current column number equal to *position*. If it is equal to the current column number then the statement has no effect, and if it is less than the current column number a new line is taken. This sets the current column number to one and the appropriate number of blanks is then output to set the current column number equal to *position*.

The following program uses *set_col* to produce exactly the same output as our earlier program.

PROGRAM 6.2

with *student_io*; **use** *student_io*;
procedure *tabulate* **is**

```
    pi : constant real := 3.141_59;
    rr : real;
begin
    --tabulate properties of sphere as radius changes
    put("radius");
    set_col(10); put("circumference");
    set_col(25); put(" volume");
    set_col(39); put_line(" surface");
    set_col(39); put_line(" of sphere");
    for r in 1 .. 10 loop
      put(r, width => 6);
      rr := real(r);
      --write circumference
      set_col(10)
      put(2.0 * pi * rr, fore => 2, aft => 3, exp => 0);
      --write volume
      set_col(25); put(4.0 / 3.0 * pi * rr ** 3, aft => 3);
      --write surface area
      set_col(39); put(4.0 * pi * rr * rr, aft => 3);
      new_line;
    end loop;
  end tabulate;
```

Although this program is longer, the connection betwen the position of the table headings and the numbers in the table can more easily be seen and controlled.

6.2 Library packages

In Ada all identifiers must be declared before they can be used. We have, however, used certain identifiers in our programs without declaring them.

We have, for example, used types such as *integer* and *character* and input and output has been performed using *put* and *get* statements. Where have these identifiers been declared?

The answer is that they have been declared in what are called "library packages". There is a "standard library package" which is automatically available to all Ada programs. It is part of the Ada language and is where the built-in types are declared.

The input and output statements are defined in a library package called *student_io*. Hence the reason why we start all our programs with

with *student_io;* **use** *student_io;*

is to make the input and output statements available to our programs.

We shall look later at the structure of packages and how we can create new ones of our own. All we need to know at present is that they can be used to hold lots of useful declarations, which can then easily be made available to Ada programs.

The package *student_io* is not part of the Ada language, but it is likely that any Ada system which is used for teaching will contain a package like it. You should find out what it is called on the system you are using and how, if at all, it differs from *student_io*. The package *student_io* is based on a more fundamental, but more difficult to use, package called *text_io* which is part of the Ada language. A description of *student_io* is given in appendix 2, together with details of the small additions which you will need to make to your programs if such a package is not available.

6.3 Predefined procedures and functions

We now know that *put*, *get*, etc. are defined in the package *student_io*, but what exactly are they?

In chapter 2 we saw that a simple Ada program consisted of a procedure. The identifiers *put*, *get*, etc. are the names of other procedures. As their definitions are complicated, they are hidden away inside a library package because, in order to be able to construct Ada programs, we do not need to know how *get* and *put* manage to read and write information; all we need to know is how to use them.

The *put*, *get*, *new_line*, *set_col* and *put_line* statements which we have used in programs are examples of what are called "procedure calls". When we have a statement like

   put(2.0 * *pi* * *rr*);

we say that we have a "call" of procedure *put*. The expression in brackets is called a "parameter". When, on the other hand, procedure *new_line* is called, it does not need a parameter and so the call is just written as

   new_line;

As well as procedures, some functions are declared in package *student_io*. Functions differ from procedures in that a call of a function returns a value. Hence a procedure call is a statement on its own while a function call is part of an expression.

One function which is available is *col*. It gives the value of the current column discussed in section 6.1. Execution of the statements

   set_col(40);
   position := *col*;

therefore first sets the current column number to 40 and then assigns this value to the variable *position*. The function *col* does not have a parameter, but many functions do.

Another useful function is *end_of_line*. This is a Boolean function, which gives the value *true* when we have read the last piece of information in a line and the value *false* at all other times.

Information typed in as data for a program and results output from a program can be considered to be a series of characters organised into lines. This line structure is modelled in Ada by means of line terminators. They are not characters in the normal sense, but they can be written and read by special procedures and recognised by the *end_of_line* function. The effect of a call of the *new_line* procedure is to write a line terminator and then to set the current column number to one. A line terminator can be read by calling the *skip_line* procedure. It causes any remaining information on the current line to be skipped and then reads the line terminator.

The following sequence of statements gives an example of how these procedures and functions can be used. We want to be able to read in five lines of data and write them out again with a line number followed by a space at the beginning of each line. It is assumed that *char* has been declared to be a character variable.

```
for line_number in 1 .. 5 loop
   put(line_number); put(' ');
   --read and write contents of a line
   while not end_of_line loop
      get(char); put(char);
   end loop;
   --deal with the line terminator
   skip_line; new_line;
end loop;
```

There is one point which may have been worrying you. The procedures *get* and *put* are sometimes called with character parameters, sometimes with integer parameters and at other times with real parameters. The reason why this is possible is that not just one *put* procedure or one *get* procedure is defined in *student_io* but several of each. The Ada system knows which one is to be used by the type of the parameter in the procedure call.

Using the same identifier to have more than one meaning is called "overloading". When we have an overloaded identifier it must always be possible for the system to work out which of the possible alternative meanings is required. As we have seen, with a procedure such as *put* it knows by the type of the parameter in the procedure call.

Until you become experienced in the use of Ada you are advised to restrict your use of overloading to the use of procedures which have been defined for your use in some library package.

6.4 Reading information

We have used *get* to read integer, real and character values. If *ch* is a character variable the effect of

> get(*ch*);

is to read the next character and assign its value to *ch*. Any leading line terminators are skipped.

If *num* is an integer variable, the effect of

> get(*num*);

is to skip any leading blanks or line terminators and then, after reading an optional plus or minus sign, to read a series of characters which represent an integer literal. The value of the integer is assigned to *num*. When *num* is a real variable the effect is the same, except that the series of characters must represent a real literal, i.e. it must include a decimal point followed by at least one digit.

Let us now consider what happens when, in response to a request to read a number, a character such as a comma is typed in. This is an example of a run-time error. When this particular kind of error occurs during execution of an Ada program, we say that "a *data_error* exception has been raised".

An exception is some event which causes suspension of the normal execution of a program. Unless steps have been taken to deal with this exceptional situation, the run-time error will cause the program to terminate. A good implementation of Ada will give useful information when this happens so that the user will be able to determine what has caused the error.

To give us some experience in handling data let us now produce a simple calculator program. The program will receive, as data, an expression like

> 3.5*4.67 + 5.39 − 2.64

and will respond by printing its value. We shall assume that the expression is to be on one line and that it contains no spaces. Evaluation is to take place from left to right with the normal precedence of operators being ignored. Brackets are not allowed.

Our first step is to produce an outline algorithm. We note that the data consists of alternating numbers and characters and the characters are to be interpreted as one of the arithmetic operators $+$, $-$, $\star$ or $/$. We also note that the data is terminated by the end of the line.

If we were to solve this problem without the aid of a computer we would go along the expression and perform the operations one by one. This would seem to suggest we have a loop, and each time round the loop calculate the "result so far". This is the loop invariant which we have to achieve.

```
read a number and make it the result so far
loop while not at the end of a line
    read an operator character
    read a number
    update the result as follows
    when the operator character is
        '+', add number to result
        '-', subtract number from result
        '/', divide result by number after checking for
            division by zero
        '*', multiply result by number
        otherwise report an error and leave loop
    end when
end loop
write the value of result
```

We must now trace this algorithm to make sure that it gives the correct answer. The first number is read and becomes the result so far. If the expression is a number alone on a line then that number is the result. Our algorithm works correctly in this case, for we go round the loop zero times. If we have more than one number then each time round the loop we read an operator followed by a number. This is used to update the value of the result. We stop when we come to the end of the line.

If we wish to be able to deal with more than one expression all we need do is enclose the above solution in an outer loop.

```
loop
    deal with an expression
    determine if we wish to continue
    exit if we do not wish to continue
end loop
```

Once we have the outline solution it is fairly straightforward to implement it in Ada:

PROGRAM 6.3

```
with student_io; use student_io;
procedure calculator is
    number, result : real;
    operator, continue : character;
begin
    loop
        put_line("Type expression");
        get(result); --result contains the answer so far
        while not end_of_line loop
            --loop also contains error exits
            --read next operator operand pair
            get(operator); get(number);
            --perform calculation
            case operator is
                when '+' =>
                    result := result + number;
                when '-' =>
                    result := result - number;
                when '/' =>
                    if number = 0.0 then
                        put_line("division by zero");
                        exit;
                    else
                        result := result / number;
                    end if;
                when '*' =>
                    result := result * number;
                when others =>
                    put_line("error in operator");
                    exit;
            end case;
            --result contains the answer so far
        end loop;
        skip_line;
        put("result = "); put(result);
        new_line;
        put("If you wish to continue type y");
        get(continue);
        exit when continue /= 'y';
    end loop;
end calculator;
```

If either a "division by zero" or "error in operator" error is
detected, the program is able, after reporting the error, to continue

and deal with the next expression. The use of *skip_line* is important here as it causes any remaining information in the error line to be skipped.

If an error is made in typing in one of the numbers in the expression then a *data_error* exception will be raised. This will cause the program to be terminated and so it will not then be possible to continue with the next expression. We shall see later how errors like this can be handled.

Exercises

1. Write a program which will produce a table of the values *n*, *n***2, *n***3, 1 / *n* and 1 / *n***2 for *n* in the range 1 to 20. The results should be in neat columns with each column having been given a suitable heading.

2. Write a program which will read in ten lines of text and will determine which line contains the largest number of the punctuation characters comma, full stop, colon or semi-colon.

3. Extend Program 6.3 so that it can deal with expressions which may contain spaces.

4. Write a series of statements to output the 95 printable characters in the ASCII character set in the order shown in appendix 3. No more than eight ASCII characters should be printed on any one line.

7

Procedures and functions

7.1 The importance of subprograms

The first step in developing programs by the method of stepwise refinement is to produce a top-level algorithm, each statement of which can be regarded as the specification of some subproblem. The solution to each subproblem is then produced by expanding the corresponding top-level statement into a series of more detailed statements, each of which can in turn be considered as the specification of a yet simpler problem.

The basic idea is that large problems are more easily solved when they are divided into a series of smaller problems which can then, to a large extent, be considered independently.

Very simple Ada programs consist of a single procedure, but we shall now see that the division of large problems into a series of smaller ones is mirrored in the way larger programs are written. Instead of producing the solution to a subproblem by expanding a top-level statement into a series of more detailed statements, we can create and then use an appropriate subprogram. There are two kinds of subprogram in Ada, namely procedures and functions, and we saw in the last chapter how predefined procedures and functions are used to perform input and output operations.

To see how we can define and use subprograms of our own, let us start with a simple example. In Program 3.4 we saw how we could draw a bordered triangle. The outline algorithm for this program might have been as follows:

        draw a border
        draw a triangle
        draw a border

The following program also draws a bordered triangle, but uses a procedure to draw the border:

PROGRAM 7.1

```
with student_io; use student_io;
procedure triangle is
   spaces : constant string := "            ";

   procedure draw_border is
      border : constant string :=
               "************************";
      begin
      --draw a two-line border surrounded by blank lines
      new_line;
      put_line(border);
      put_line(border);
      new_line;
   end draw_border;

   begin
   --print a bordered triangle
   draw_border;
   put(spaces); put_line("  *");
   put(spaces); put_line(" ***");
   put(spaces); put_line("*****");
   draw_border;
end triangle;
```

In this program we have two procedures, one of which, procedure *triangle*, acts as the "main program". Within the declarative part of procedure *triangle* we have the declaration of a "procedure body" called *draw_border*. The instructions to draw the border are contained in the sequence of statements within this procedure body.

To see how the program produces the bordered triangle, let us trace its execution. After any initialisation of variables in the declarative part of the main program, execution of an Ada program begins with the first statement in the main program. In our example this is a call of the procedure *draw_border* and so this procedure is entered and the statements in it are executed. This causes two lines of asterisks surrounded by blank lines to be output.

Once this has been done we leave the procedure and return to the statement following the original procedure call. This and the following statements cause a triangle to be printed.

We then come to the statement

   draw_border;

This is the second call of procedure *draw_border* and once again we enter the procedure, obey the statements in the procedure body, and then leave the procedure and return to the main program. As we are now at the end of the program, execution stops.

Let us examine what we have done. Several statements, whose combined effect is to draw a border, have been grouped into a procedure and given a name. Now, if we wish to draw a border, all we need do is call this procedure. While we were constructing the procedure we concentrated on how we could draw a border. Once the procedure has been written and tested so that we are sure it is working correctly, we do not need to bother about the details of how it works, just as we do not need to bother about how the predefined procedures *get* and *put* manage to read and write information. What we are now interested in is how we can use the procedure. We require the specification of what it does rather than how it does it.

To look at it from another angle, we can consider that, when a subprogram has been written to solve a subproblem, a new basic operation has been added to our programming language.

7.2 Local declarations

We have seen how variables, constants, types and subprogram bodies can be declared in the declarative part of our main program procedure. They can be declared in the declarative part of procedure bodies such as *draw_border* in exactly the same way. Hence in our example the declaration of the constant called *border* took place within procedure *draw_border*.

This is an example of a local declaration. As *border* has been declared inside procedure *draw_border*, it is defined only within the procedure. We say that it is "local to the procedure". The main program has never heard of a constant called *border*.

Let us now consider the declaration of the constant called *spaces*. It is declared in the main program and is used in the main program. This constant can be used within procedure *draw_border*, as identifiers declared in the main program are visible inside an inner procedure. Identifiers declared outside a procedure and visible inside it are said to be "global" or "non-local" to the procedure.

We could have declared *border* in the main program and still used it inside procedure *draw_border*. It is, however, good practice to declare identifiers as locally as possible so that their declarations and use are kept together. This helps to keep procedures as self-contained as possible. When different sections of a program are relatively independent they can be written and tested separately. It also makes it easier to re-use a procedure which has been written as part of one program when we are constructing another program. In this way we do not have continually to re-invent the wheel. For these reasons the use of global identifiers should be kept to a minimum.

There is one important point to mention about the order of declarations in a declarative part. The order in which types, variables and constants are declared does not matter as long as identifiers are declared before they are used, but they must all be declared before the declaration of any subprogram bodies.

7.3 Parameters

Procedure *draw_border* in Program 7.1 is not very flexible because it can only draw a border of a certain size. What makes procedures really useful and flexible is the use of parameters. Let us see how procedure *draw_border* can be extended so that, instead of always printing a border of 25 asterisks, it could produce a border of any specified width.

PROGRAM 7.2

```
with student_io; use student_io;
procedure triangle is
  spaces : constant string := "          ";

  procedure draw_border(width : in integer) is
  begin
    --draw a two-line border surrounded by blank lines
    --there are width asterisks in each border line
    new_line;
    for border_line in 1 .. 2 loop
      --write width asterisks
      for asterisks in 1 .. width loop
        put('*');
      end loop;
      new_line;
    end loop;
    new_line;
  end draw_border;

begin
  --print a bordered triangle
  draw_border(25);
  put(spaces); put_line("  *");
  put(spaces); put_line(" ***");
  put(spaces); put_line("*****");
  draw_border(25);
end triangle;
```

In the definition of the procedure body of *draw_border* we have a "formal parameter" called *width*. It is of type *integer*. The reserved word **in** gives the "mode" of the parameter. As it is **in**, this means that the parameter is used to pass information into the procedure. We shall come across other modes later.

When we call the procedure we have to give a value to the formal parameter by means of an "actual parameter". In the procedure call

> *draw_border*(25);

the value 25 is the actual parameter. The types of the actual and formal parameters must match. Formal parameters of **in** mode are constants and so, after they have been given a value during the procedure call, that value cannot be changed during execution of the procedure.

Let us now see what happens when the program is executed. We begin at the first statement in the main program. It is

> *draw_border*(25);

This causes procedure *draw_border* to be entered. The actual parameter 25 is passed into the procedure and is associated with the formal parameter *width*, i.e. *width* is given the value 25.

The statements in the procedure are now executed and, after a blank line has been output, the nested loops cause two lines of asterisks to be printed, each of length 25. Another blank line is then output.

We then return from *draw_border* to the main program, where the triangle is printed before we once again enter *draw_border*, where a second border is output. On leaving the second execution of *draw_border* we return to the main program and execution stops.

The action of this new version of *draw_border* depends on the value of the actual parameter. Note also that although *draw_border* now produces the border in a different way, the user of the procedure need not be aware of this. All the user need know is how to call the procedure and its net effect.

As our new version of *draw_border* is more complicated than the previous one and the same constant actual parameter was used in both procedure calls, we appear to have lost more than we have gained. However the advantages should become clear in the following extension to our problem.

Our present triangle program prints out a bordered three-line triangle as follows:

```
*************************
*************************

            *
           ***
          *****

*************************
*************************
```

Let us extend the problem to that of producing a triangle of any size, where the size of a triangle is defined to be the number of lines it occupies. The triangle will still have ten spaces to its left and be centred within a border of asterisks.

Our initial outline algorithm might be

> get triangle size
> draw suitable border
> draw triangle of the appropriate size
> draw suitable border

We must now consider the question of the size of the triangle. If the triangle is to be output on *size* lines then the number of asterisks in its base will be

> $2 * size - 1$

Because it has ten asterisks on each side of the triangle, the width of the border is "the length of the triangle base + 20".

Using this information, our next version of the outline algorithm becomes

> get triangle size
> calculate length of triangle base
> draw border of width "20 + triangle base"
> draw triangle on "size" lines
> draw border of width "20 + triangle base"

As we already have a procedure which can draw a border of any given size, all we need do is solve the subproblem

> draw triangle on "size" lines

Let us now consider this problem. On the first line of the triangle, one asterisk is printed and on each subsequent line the number of asterisks is increased by two. We have still to work out the initial number of leading spaces, but we note that the number of leading spaces on each line is one less than the line before. This leads to the following outline algorithm:

set number of asterisks to 1
initialise the space counter
loop "size" times
    output the appropriate number of spaces
    print the appropriate number of asterisks
    decrement the space counter by 1
    increment the asterisk counter by 2
    output a line terminator
end loop

Putting these different components together gives us the following program. It uses a procedure to draw the actual triangle.

PROGRAM 7.3

```ada
with student_io; use student_io;
procedure triangle is
   triangle_base, triangle_size : integer;

   procedure draw_border(width : in integer) is
   begin
      --draw a two-line border surrounded by blank lines
      --there are width asterisks in each border line
      new_line;
      for border_line in 1 .. 2 loop
         --write width asterisks
         for asterisks in 1 .. width loop
            put('*');
         end loop;
         end_line;
      end loop;
      new_line;
   end draw_border;

   procedure draw_triangle(number_lines : in integer) is
      space_counter : integer := 10 + number_lines - 1;
      num_asterisks : integer := 1;
   begin
      --draw triangle on number_lines lines
      for lines in 1 .. number_lines loop
         --write leading spaces
         for spaces in 1 .. space_counter loop
            put(' ');
         end loop;
         --write asterisks
         for asterisks in 1 .. num_asterisks loop
            put('*');
```

```
        end loop;
        new_line;
        space_counter := space_counter - 1;
        num_asterisks := num_asterisks + 2;
      end loop;
    end draw_triangle;

begin
    --print a bordered triangle on triangle_size lines
    put("How many lines in the triangle?"); get(triangle_size);
    triangle_base := 2 * triangle_size - 1;
    draw_border(20 + triangle_base);
    draw_triangle(triangle_size);
    draw_border(20 + triangle_base);
end triangle;
```

Note how short our main program has become and how closely it matches our outline algorithm. We shall find that it is often the case that statements in an outline algorithm are implemented as procedure calls. Because we have chosen meaningful names for our procedures it is possible, just by reading the statements in the main program, to gain a very good idea about what the program does.

Now that we have examined several procedures let us look at the general structure of a subprogram body. This is best shown by its syntax diagram

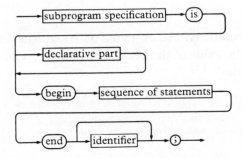

where, for a procedure, the subprogram specification is

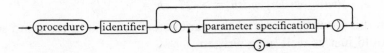

7.4 **Positional, named and default parameters**

Procedure *draw_border* always prints a border of asterisks. Let us now modify it so that it can print a border consisting of any specified character. The procedure body becomes

```
procedure draw_border(width : in integer; ch : in character) is
begin
   --draw a two-line border surrounded by blank lines
   --there are width characters in each border line
   new_line;
   for border_line in 1 .. 2 loop
      --write width characters
      for chars in 1 .. width loop
         put(ch);
      end loop;
      new_line;
   end loop;
   new_line;
end draw_border;
```

This procedure has two formal parameters *width* and *ch*, both of **in** mode. A call of this procedure must have two actual parameters. The first actual parameter is associated with the first formal parameter and so it must be of type *integer*; the second actual parameter is associated with the second formal parameter and so it must be a character. A possible procedure call is

```
draw_border(25, '%');
```

After such a call the procedure will be executed with *width* having the value 25 and *ch* having the value of the per cent character. The effect will be to print the border

%%%%%%%%%%%%%%%%%%%%%%%%%

%%%%%%%%%%%%%%%%%%%%%%%%%

As an alternative to this "positional" form of matching formal and actual parameters, we can use a longer "named" form in which the formal parameters are stated explicitly in the procedure call, as in

```
draw_border(width = > 25, ch = > '%');
```

In this form the order of the parameters does not matter and so we could just as well have written

```
draw_border(ch = > '%', width = > 25);
```

It is possible to mix the positional and named forms, but in such a case the positional form must come first, i.e. we can write

   draw_border(25, *ch* = > '%');

but here the order is important.

The named notation is the one we used when specifying the layout conventions with the predefined procedure *put*. You will also remember that when we used *put* the number of actual parameters could vary. Hence, with *num* of type *real*, we could have the following calls:

   put(*num*, *fore* = > 5, *aft* = > 6, *exp* = > 2);
   put(*num*, *fore* = > 4);
   put(*num*);

How is this possible?

Just as variables can be initialised when they are declared, parameters of **in** mode can be given a default initial value, as can be seen from the (simplified) syntax diagram for a parameter specification:

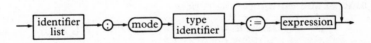

If we want our *draw_border* procedure normally to print asterisks, but to have the ability to print other characters, it could be declared as

   procedure *draw_border*(*width* : **in** *integer*;
                    ch : **in** *character* := '*') **is**

   . . .

   end *draw_border*;

We can call the procedure as

   draw_border(25, '%');

in which case it will print a border of per cent characters, but, as the formal parameter *ch* has been given a default value, a call of the procedure with only one parameter

   draw_border(25);

has the same effect as the call

   draw_border(25, '*');

The *fore*, *aft* and *exp* formal parameters in the definition of *put* all have default values. The *new_line* procedure also has a default parameter to control the number of new lines to be taken. The default value is one, but if we want more we can have a call such as

   new_line(3);

When an actual parameter is omitted from a call and its default value used, all subsequent parameters in the call must use the named form of parameter association. With the *put* procedure, the value being printed comes first and so the positional notation can be used for it. However, because it is far from easy to remember the order in which they are declared, it is safer to use named association for the other parameters even when none are omitted.

7.5 Functions

Function subprograms differ from procedures in that they return a value. Hence a procedure call is a statement while a function call is part of an expression. In chapter 6 we saw how to use predefined functions such as *col* and *end_of_line*. Let us now look at how a function body can be declared.

As an example, let us create a function called *next_day* which, given a value of the enumeration type

  type *day* **is** (*sun*, *mon*, *tues*, *wed*, *thurs*, *fri*, *sat*);

will calculate the following day. The declaration is

  function *next_day*(*this_day* : **in** *day*) **return** *day* **is**
  begin
   if *this_day* = *day'last* **then**
    return *day'first*;
   else
    return *day'succ*(*this_day*);
   end if;
  end *next_day*;

Because functions return a value, the type of this value must be given in the subprogram specification. The type is given after the reserved word **return** and in this case is type *day*.

Execution of a function is terminated by executing a statement of the form

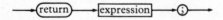

The value of the expression is returned to the calling program and must be of the type given in the subprogram specification. Only parameters of **in** mode can be used with functions.

If *today* and *tomorrow* are two variables of type *day* and *today* has been given the value *thurs*, the effect of executing the statement

   tomorrow := *next_day(today)*;

will be to give *tomorrow* the value *fri*.

   Another function is shown in the following program, which reads in a number of yards, feet and inches and prints the corresponding number of metres. The actual conversion is performed by a function which accepts three integer parameters and returns a real value.

PROGRAM 7.4

```
with student_io, use student_io;
procedure convert is
   yards, feet, inches : integer;
   metres : real;

   function no_of_metres(yds, ft, ins : in integer) return real is
      inches : integer;
      inches_to_metres : constant real := 0.02540;
   begin
      --convert yds, ft and ins to metres
      inches := yds * 36 + ft * 12 + ins;
      return real(inches) * inches_to_metres;
   end no_of_metres;

begin
   --read number of yards, feet and inches
   put("yards?"); get(yards);
   put("feet?"); get(feet);
   put("inches?"); get(inches);
   --calculate and print corresponding number of metres
   metres := no_of_metres(yards, feet, inches);
   put("number of metres =");
   put(metres, aft => 3, exp => 0);
   new_line;
end convert;
```

   You will notice that in this program an integer variable called *inches* is declared in the function, while another integer variable called *inches* is declared in the main program. They are two completely different variables. Within the main program any reference to *inches* refers to the identifier declared in the main program and within the function any reference to *inches* refers to the identifier declared in the function. The rule is that the most local declaration always takes precedence over any other declaration.

   As we have seen, the definition of a procedure body and the

definition of a function body differ in the form of the subprogram specification. The subprogram specification for a procedure has already been given. For a function the (simplified) syntax diagram is

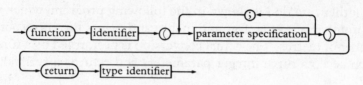

7.6 **Parameter modes** out **and** in out

Our example procedures and functions have shown how parameters can be used to pass information into a subprogram. It is often useful to pass information into a procedure, have it modified within the procedure and then have the modified information passed back to the calling routine.

Consider the following program, where we have a procedure with two parameters of mode **in out**:

PROGRAM 7.5

```
with student_io; use student_io;
procedure order is
  smaller, larger : real;

  procedure swap(first, second : in out real) is
    old_first : real;
  begin
    --swap the values of the two parameters
    old_first := first;
    first := second;
    second := old_first;
  end swap;

begin
  --read and order two numbers
  get(smaller); get(larger);
  if smaller > larger then
    swap(smaller, larger);
  end if;
  put("The ordered numbers are: ");
  put(smaller); put(larger);
  new_line;
end order;
```

In procedure *swap* we have two real formal parameters of mode **in out** and one local variable. Execution of the program begins with two numbers being read and assigned to *smaller* and *larger*. If the value of *smaller* is greater than the value of *larger*, we enter procedure *swap*.

The types of the corresponding actual and formal parameters must match. During execution of the procedure, **in out** formal parameters act as local variables which have been initialised to the value of the corresponding actual parameter. Hence *first* is initially given the value of the actual parameter *smaller* and *second* is given the value of the actual parameter *larger*.

The statements in the procedure are then executed causing the values of *first* and *second* to be swapped. We now leave the procedure and, because *first* and *second* are of mode **in out**, the current value of *first* is assigned to the actual parameter *smaller* and the current value of *second* is assigned to the actual parameter *larger*.

The effect of executing procedure *swap* is therefore to swap the values of the variables *smaller* and *larger*.

With **in out** (and **out**) parameters the actual parameters must be variables as they are updated by the procedure call. With **in** parameters information is only passed into the procedure and so the actual parameters can be expressions. If we wish a procedure to change the value of an actual parameter then the formal parameters must either be of mode **in out** or **out**.

Parameters of mode **out** are undefined when execution of the procedure starts. They must be given a value during execution of the procedure and, on leaving the procedure, this value is assigned to the actual parameter. Even after they have been given a value, formal parameters of mode **out** may not be used in an expression. Their only appearance within a procedure is when they are being given a value.

We therefore use **in** mode parameters to pass information into a procedure, **out** mode parameters to receive information from a procedure and **in out** mode parameters to pass in information which can be changed before being passed back out again. When the mode of a parameter is not specified it is taken to be **in**.

The following procedure uses an **out** mode parameter. Fairly frequently there are restrictions on the range of acceptable numbers which may be read into a program. The following procedure could be used when only positive numbers were acceptable. If a negative number is read, an error message is printed and the user is then prompted to make a second attempt.

```
procedure read_pos(number : out real) is
   any_value : real;
begin
   --read numbers until a positive number is obtained
```

```
loop
    put("positive number please:");
    get(any_value);
    if any_value < 0.0 then
        put_line("error: number must be positive");
    else
        number := any_value;
        return;
    end if;
end loop;
end read_pos;
```

This procedure shows another use of the return statement. A procedure may be left either by executing a return statement or by coming to the end of the sequence of statements in the procedure body. As procedures do not return a value, there is no expression following the reserved word **return**.

Functions must always be left by the execution of a return statement.

7.7   Example problem

Let us now consider the problem of reading an integer number and writing it out in English, i.e. converting a number such as 647 to "six hundred and fortyseven". We shall assume that only members in the range − 999 999 to 999 999 are to be dealt with.

If we develop the solution by the method of stepwise refinement, a first attempt might lead us to the following simple algorithm:

```
read a number
if the number is negative then
    write "minus"
    make the number positive
end if
write a positive number in English
```

This has not got us very far, but we are now able to concentrate on the main part of the problem, which is to write out, in English, the value of a positive number. Our next step is to look for patterns in the way numbers are written. Consider the number 234 567. In English this is "two hundred and thirtyfour thousand five hundred and sixtyseven". We note that the number of thousands is written in the same way as the part under a thousand. This leads to

```
if the number is greater than 999 then
    write the number of thousands
```

```
      write "thousand"
   end if
   write the part under a thousand
```

This has reduced the problem to that of writing a number in the range 1 to 999. A first attempt at this might be

```
   if number is greater than 99 then
      write number of hundreds
      write "hundred"
   end if
   if number of tens is greater than zero then
      write number of tens
   end if
   write last digit unless it is zero
```

The remaining problem of being given a number in the range 1 to 9 and writing "one", "two", etc. is easily solved.

We now have a general approach to the solution, although some problems remain. For example, numbers in the range 10 to 19 are written in a non-standard way and not as "onetynine", etc. This will require a change in the algorithm, but this can be achieved without spoiling the basic structure. You will find that initial solutions often require modifications like this; it is very important for these changes to be made at the design stage rather than during the implementation.

The last four lines of our algorithm should be changed to

```
   if number of tens is one then
      write the English for the last two digits
   else
      if number of tens is greater than one then
         write number of tens
      end if
      write last digit unless it is zero
   end if
```

Once an overall design for a program has been produced, we can start implementing it in Ada. The design was produced "from the top down", but that does not mean that it has to be implemented in this way. Large programs are often implemented in small pieces, which are compiled and tested separately before being combined.

Our first step in implementing the program might be to write and test a procedure to deal with a number in the range 0 to 9. If the number is zero nothing will be written, otherwise "one", "two", etc. will be written as appropriate. The following program can be used to test the procedure:

PROGRAM 7.6

```ada
with student_io; use student_io;
procedure write_number is
  number : integer;

  procedure write_digit(digit : in integer) is
  begin
    --write number in the range 1 to 9
    case digit is
      when 1 = > put("one");
      when 2 = > put("two");
      when 3 = > put("three");
      when 4 = > put("four");
      when 5 = > put("five");
      when 6 = > put("six");
      when 7 = > put("seven");
      when 8 = > put("eight");
      when 9 = > put("nine");
      when others = > null;
    end case;
  end write_digit;

begin
  put("number please"); get(number);
  if number < 0 then
    --deal with negative number
    put("minus ");
    number := -number;
  end if;
  if number < 10 then
    write_digit(number);
  else
    put("number too large");
  end if;
  new_line;
end write_number;
```

When, in the case statement, *digit* is outside the range 1 to 9 we want no action to be taken. This is indicated by the use of the "null statement", which is just written as

null;

Execution of a null statement has no effect, but it is necessary to show that we have made a positive decision to do nothing and have not just forgotten about the possibility of *digit* being outside the range 1 to 9.

Once this part of the program has been thoroughly tested we can continue with the implementation of the rest of the design. This might involve an intermediate stage that deals with numbers up to 99.

The approach of implementing the solution in stages is often called "incremental implementation". The advantage is that at each stage we need to test only a relatively small new piece of code, for most of the program will already have been tested at an earlier stage. A program to solve the complete problem is now given.

PROGRAM 7.7

```
with student_io; use student_io;
procedure write_number is
    number : integer;

    procedure write_1_to_999(num : in integer) is
        under_100 : constant integer := num rem 100;

        procedure write_digit(digit : in integer) is
        begin
            --write number in the range 1 to 9
            case digit is
                when 1 => put("one");
                when 2 => put("two");
                when 3 => put("three");
                when 4 => put("four");
                when 5 => put("five");
                when 6 => put("six");
                when 7 => put("seven");
                when 8 => put("eight");
                when 9 => put("nine");
                when others => null;
            end case;
        end write_digit

        procedure write_tens(tens : in integer) is
        begin
            --deal with twenty to ninety
            case tens is
                when 2 => put("twenty");
                when 3 => put("thirty");
                when 4 => put("forty");
                when 5 => put("fifty");
                when 8 => put("eighty");
                when others => write_digit(tens);
                                put("ty");
            end case;
        end write_tens;
```

```ada
begin
  --write numbers in range 1 to 999
  if num > 99 then
    --write number of hundreds
    write_digit(num / 100);
    put(" hundred");
    if under_100 /= 0 then
      --and required if anything after hundred
      put(" and");
    end if;
  end if;
  if under_100 in 10 .. 19 then
    --deal with 10 to 19
    case under_100 is
      when 10 = > put("ten");
      when 11 = > put("eleven");
      when 12 = > put("twelve");
      when 13 = > put("thirteen");
      when 15 = > put("fifteen");
      when 18 = > put("eighteen");
      when others = > write_digit(under_100 rem 10);
                      put("teen");
    end case;
  else
    if under_100 > = 20 then
      --write tens part
      write_tens(under_100 / 10);
    end if;
    --write digits part
    write_digit(under_100 rem 10);
  end if;
end write_1_to_999;

begin
  --write number in the range - 999999 to 999999
  put("number please"); get(number);
  if number < 0 then
    --deal with negative number
    put("minus ");
    number := - number;
  end if;
  if number > 999_999 then
    put("number too large");
  elsif number = 0 then
    --zero is a special case
    put("zero");
```

```
    else
      if number > 999 then
      --deal with number of thousands
         write_1_to_999(number / 1000);
         put(" thousand ");
         number := number rem 1000;
         if number in 1 .. 99 then
            put("and ");
         end if;
      end if;
      --deal with part under 1000
      write_1_to_999(number);
    end if;
    new_line;
  end write_number;
```

Note that in this program the two procedures *write_digit* and *write_tens* are declared locally within procedure *write_1_to_999*. These two procedures could have been declared in the declarative part of the main program, but declaring them in the declarative part of *write_1_to_999* means that the procedure *write_1_to_999* remains self-contained.

7.8 Recursion

Apart from the fact that a subprogram must be declared before it can be called, there are no restrictions on the position of subprogram calls. A subprogram can even call itself. This is known as a recursive call and is useful when the solution to a problem can be expressed in terms of a simpler version of the same problem.

The usual example of this is the calculation of factorials. The definition of, for example, four factorial (written as 4!) is

$$4 \times 3 \times 2 \times 1$$

while in general we have

$$n! = n \times (n - 1) \times \ldots \times 2 \times 1$$

Examination of the definition shows that 4! can be expressed as $4 \times 3!$, i.e. we can define 4! in terms of 3!. Similarly 3! can be defined in terms of 2! and 2! in terms of 1!, whose value we already know, for it is just 1. In general we can define $n!$ in terms of $(n - 1)!$.

This approach of defining a factorial in terms of a simpler version of itself can be used in the construction of a factorial function.

```
    function factorial(n : integer) return integer is
    begin
```

```
--n must be non-negative
if n > 1 then
   return n * factorial(n − 1);
else
   return 1;
end if;
end factorial;
```

Within the body of function *factorial* we have a call of function *factorial*. This is an example of a recursive call and we say that *factorial* is a recursive function.

Let us now consider the call

  factorial(4);

When the function is entered the **in** parameter *n* is given the value 4. Because this is greater than 1, the expression

  4 * *factorial*(3)

is evaluated and its value returned as the value of the function. Evaluation of this expression involves a recursive call of the function, namely the call *factorial*(3). Evaluation of *factorial*(3) will require the call *factorial*(2), which in turn will require the call *factorial*(1). The secret is that each of these calls is simpler than the one before until eventually we have a call of the function, namely *factorial*(1), which does not require any further recursive calls and just returns the value 1.

The value of the expression

  2 * *factorial*(1)

is therefore 2, the value of the expression

  3 * *factorial*(2)

is 6 and the value of

  4 * *factorial*(3)

is 24. The value returned by the call

  factorial(4);

is therefore 24.

It is essential with recursive subprograms that, as in this example, the recursion eventually stops. Otherwise we have "infinite recursion", which is the recursive counterpart of the infinite loop.

There are many problems whose simplest and most elegant solution involves recursive procedures or functions.

7.9 **Summary**

Now that we have seen how procedures can be used, let us summarise the benefits. Our approach to the solution to large problems has been to divide them into a series of fairly independent smaller problems. When procedures are used in the implementation of the solution to these subproblems we produce, not one large monolithic program, but a collection of related subprograms.

As the subprograms are relatively independent they can be written and tested separately. Large programs can then be built up from smaller ones which have already been written and tested.

Also, the solutions to many seemingly unrelated problems often have common features. Subprograms written and tested as part of the solution to one problem may be of direct use in the implementation of solutions to other problems. This leads us to the notion of having libraries of useful subprograms. This is an important feature of Ada, which has facilities to support the creation and use of program libraries. We shall return to this topic later.

Finally, procedures allow us to define new "higher-level" operations which can help us think about the solution to problems by removing unwanted detail.

Exercises

1. Consider the following program:

```
with student_io; use student_io;
procedure factors is
   large, small : integer;

   function hcf(low, high : integer) return integer is
      remainder : integer;
      bigger : integer := high;
      smaller : integer := low;
   begin
      --find the highest common factor
      loop
         remainder := bigger rem smaller;
         exit when remainder = 0;
         bigger := smaller;
         smaller := remainder;
      end loop;
      return smaller;
   end hcf;
```

```
begin
    put_line("input two positive integers, the smaller first");
    get(small); get(large);
    if small < large and small > 0 then
        put("Their highest common factor is ");
        put(hcf(small, large), width = > 1); new_line;
    else
        put_line("The data has the wrong format");
    end if;
end factors;
```

Identify each of the following in the program: a formal parameter, an actual parameter, a function call, a procedure call and a local declaration.

Rewrite the function call using the named form of passing parameters.

Trace the execution of the program when the input data is
21 35

Add to the function comments to describe the loop invariant.

2. Consider the following function:

```
function increase(number : integer; by : integer := 1)
    return integer is
begin
    return number + by;
end increase;
```

What would be the effect of executing each of the following function calls?

```
val := increase(3);
val := increase(3, 1);
val := increase(3, 2);
val := increase(3, by = > 4);
val := increase(by = > 4, number = > 3);
```

3. Procedure *swap* in section 7.6 exchanges the values of two real variables. Rewrite the procedure so that it will exchange the values of two variables of type *day*.

4. In section 7.5 function *next_day* is defined. Write an analogous function called *previous_day*.

5. Extend Program 7.7 so that it will write, in English, numbers in the range -999_999_999 to 999_999_999.

6. Write a procedure which, when given as parameters the number of days in a month and the day of the week on which

the month starts, will write out a calendar for the month in the form

```
Su M  Tu W  Th F   Sa
                 1   2
 3   4   5   6   7   8   9
10  11  12  13  14  15  16
17  18  19  20  21  22  23
24  25  26  27  28  29  30
31
```

Write a program which, when given the number of days in a year and the day of the week of the first of January, will produce a 12-month calendar.

7. What would be the effect of executing the statement

   put(hcf(21,35));

   where *hcf* has been declared as

   function *hcf(low, high : integer)* **return** *integer* **is**
      remainder : integer := high **rem** *low*;
   begin
      if *remainder* = 0 **then**
        return *low*;
      else
        return *hcf(remainder, low)*;
      end if;
   end *hcf*;

   Compare the execution of this function with the execution of the function declared in question 1.

8

Declarations re-visited

8.1 Subtype declarations

It is common in programming to have variables whose values will, if the program works as expected, never go outside a certain range. If we had, for example, a variable *today* which was declared to be of type *day*

type *day* **is** (*sun, mon, tues, wed, thurs, fri, sat*);

but which should only take values in the range *mon* to *fri* then, instead of declaring it to be of type *day*, it would be useful to be able to declare it as a subrange or subtype of *day* and have its values restricted to the required range.

This can be done by replacing the declaration

today : *day*;

by the declaration

today : *day* **range** *mon .. fri*;

Alternatively, we can give a name to the subtype by means of a subtype declaration

subtype *weekday* **is** *day* **range** *mon .. fri*;

and then declare the variable *today* to be of the subtype *weekday*

today : *weekday*;

A subtype is therefore created from an existing type or subtype by restricting the set of allowed values.

The general form of a subtype declaration is

where a subtype indication is defined by

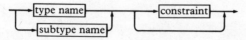

The constraint used in the above example is called a "range constraint". Having information about the range of expected values included in a program has two advantages. It makes it clear to a reader of the program what our intentions are, and this should help in their understanding of the program. Secondly, if, due to some logical error, we try to assign to *today* a value which is outside the allowed range this will be picked up by the system. Exceptions were introduced in chapter 6 and we saw how a *data_error* exception could be raised. If a range constraint is violated at run-time then a *constraint_error* exception is raised. Our ability to trap incorrect programs is therefore increased.

When you start programming, a feature which can lead to the system finding more errors may not seem attractive, but there is nothing worse than having an error lurking in your program. Sooner or later it is sure to manifest itself at the most inopportune moment. Because our aim is to produce correct programs, we want to have as much help as we can from the system in showing up any logical flaws so that they can be corrected.

No flexibility is lost by using subtypes. Any operations available with the original type (called the "base type") can be used with the subtype, and objects of a given subtype can be used in expressions wherever objects of the base type can be used.

Subtype names can be used wherever type names can be used. In Ada they are often both referred to as "type marks". We can, for example, have subtypes of subtypes. Using the definition of *weekday* given above, we could have

    subtype *early_weekday* **is** *weekday* **range** *mon .. wed*;

It would, of course, have been an error if the range constraint of *early_weekday* had not been within the range constraint of *weekday*.

Type marks can be used in the test of whether or not a variable is within a certain range. Hence if *tomorrow* is a variable of type *day*, the three Boolean expressions

    tomorrow **in** *mon .. fri*
    tomorrow **in** *weekday'first .. weekday'last*
    tomorrow **in** *weekday*

are all identical in their effect.

It is often the case in a program that an integer variable should never be negative. This occurs so frequently that Ada has two built-in integer subtypes:

    subtype *natural* **is** 0 *.. integer'last*;

subtype *positive* **is** 1 .. *integer'last*;

Some of the programs in previous chapters can be modified to use variables of subtype *positive* or *natural* instead of type *integer*. You are recommended to go over these programs and decide where this change can be made and where it cannot.

As an example of the use of subtypes, let us consider the following function, which accepts two primary colours and returns the result of mixing them together. We shall assume that the declarations

type *colour* **is** (*red, yellow, blue, purple, green, orange*);
subtype *primary* **is** *colour* **range** *red* .. *blue*;

have already been made.

```
function mix(prim_1, prim_2 : in primary) return colour is
begin
    --mix two primary colours
    if prim_1 = prim_2 then
        return prim_1;
    end if;
    case prim_1 is
        when red = >
            if prim_2 = blue then
                return purple;
            else
                return orange;
            end if;
        when blue = >
            if prim_2 = red then
                return purple;
            else
                return green;
            end if;
        when yellow = >
            if prim_2 = red then
                return orange;
            else
                return green;
            end if;
    end case;
end mix;
```

There is no return statement at the end of the function because every possible path through the function has already been terminated by a return statement.

In a case statement there must be a choice for each possible value the case expression can take, but as the parameter *prim_1* is of the subtype *primary* only the cases *red*, *yellow* and *blue* have to be catered for in this example.

Care must be taken when using subtypes. Consider for example what would happen if we had the declarations

subtype *small_int* **is** *integer* **range** 1 .. 10;
count : *small_int* := 1;
sum : *natural* := 0;

and tried to use the following code to sum the numbers from 1 to 10:

while *count* < = 10 **loop**
  sum := *sum* + *count*;
  count := *count* + 1;
end loop;

On the tenth iteration round the loop, execution of the statement

count := *count* + 1;

attempts to give *count* the value 11 which is, of course, out of range.

8.2 Attributes of discrete types

In chapter 4 the attributes *first*, *last*, *succ* and *pred* were introduced. As you might expect, they are defined for subtypes as well as for types, and we have already used the *first* and *last* attributes of *weekday*.

Now that we have dealt with functions we can see that the *succ* and *pred* attributes are single parameter functions. The only really new point to note is that if we have the declarations

working : *weekday* := *fri*;
holiday : *day*;

then the assignment

holiday := *weekday'succ(working)*;

is perfectly legal and *holiday* will be given the value *sat*. A *constraint_error* would, however, have been raised if the assignment

working := *weekday'succ(working)*;

had been attempted or if an attempt to evaluate *day'succ(sat)* or *day'pred(sun)* had been made.

Several other attributes are available. The position of an enumeration value in its declaration (with the count starting at zero) is given by the *pos* attribute. Hence we have

day'pos(sun) = 0
day'pos(mon) = 1

This operation can be carried out in the reverse direction using the *val* attribute. Hence

day'val(3) = *wed*
day'val(4) = *thurs*

An attempt to evaluate *day'val*(7) would raise a *constraint_error* exception.

The *pos* and *val* attributes have the same effect with a subtype as they do with its base type. Hence, for example, *weekday'val*(6) is legal and gives the value *sat*.

You should not make extensive use of the *pos* and *val* attributes, but they can be useful on occasion. Consider the following statement, in which it has been assumed that *ch* and *num* have been declared to be character and integer variables respectively:

> **if** *ch* **in** '0' .. '9' **then**
>   *num* := *character'pos*(*ch*) − *character'pos*('0');
> **end if**;

The *pos* attribute of a character value is its position in the ASCII character set. Because the digit characters are in consecutive positions in ASCII, if *ch* is equal to one of the digit characters '0' to '9' then execution of the above statement puts its integer equivalent in *num*.

Another useful attribute is *image*. The value of *day'image*(*sun*) is the string "SUN". Hence the *image* attribute converts an enumeration value into a sequence of upper case characters. This allows an enumeration value to be written out as a string. The value of *integer'image*(34) is the string " 34". The string image of an integer contains either a leading space or a minus sign.

Conversely the attribute *day'value*("SUN") has the value *sun*. This allows us to convert a string into a value of a specified type. The value of *integer'value*("34") is the integer 34.

Associated with *image* is the *width* attribute. It gives the maximum image width for a type or subtype. Hence *day'width* has the value 5 as the longest string image is that corresponding to the enumeration value *thurs*.

Let us now see how we can use the image attribute to give a very different solution to our earlier problem of printing the value of a number in English. This time we shall restrict ourselves to numbers in the range −99 to 99, but the solution can easily be extended.

PROGRAM 8.1

```
with student_io; use student_io;
procedure write_number is
```

```
type zero_to_19 is (zero, one, two, three, four, five, six, seven,
                    eight, nine, ten, eleven, twelve, thirteen,
                    fourteen, fifteen, sixteen, seventeen, eighteen,
                    nineteen);
subtype zero_to_nine is zero_to_19 range zero .. nine;
low_val : zero_to_19;
digit : zero_to_nine;
type tens is (place_0, place_1, twenty, thirty, forty, fifty, sixty,
              seventy, eighty, ninety);
tens_part : tens;
number : integer;
begin
--write numbers in the range -99 to 99
put("number please"); get(number);
if number < 0 then
   --deal with negative number
   put("minus ");
   number := -number:
end if;
if number > 99 then
   put("number too large");
elsif number < = 19 then
   --convert number to enumeration value and write its image
   low_val := zero_to_19'val(number);
   put(zero_to_19'image(low_val));
else
   --deal with numbers from 20 to 99
   --find tens part and write its image
   tens_part := tens'val(number / 10);
   put(tens'image(tens_part));
   --find digit part and write its image if nonzero
   digit := zero_to_nine'val(number rem 10);
   if digit /= zero then
      put(zero_to_nine'image(digit));
   end if;
end if;
new_line;
end write_number;
```

Let us trace the execution of this program so that we can see what is happening. We shall assume that 37 has been read in as data and has been assigned to *number*. Checks are made to find if it is less than 0, greater than 99 or less than or equal to 19. All these tests fail and so we enter the else part, where the statement

```
tens_part := tens'val(number / 10);
```

is to be executed. Dividing 37 by 10 gives the value 3 and the result of evaluating *tens'val*(3) is the enumeration value *thirty*, which is assigned to the variable *tens_part*. The effect of executing the statement

   put(*tens'image*(*tens_part*));

is therefore to print the string

   THIRTY

The enumeration values *place_0* and *place_1* are dummy values to ensure the correct positioning of *twenty*, *thirty*, etc.

   Execution of the program continues with the enumeration value *seven* being assigned to the variable *digit*. As it is not *zero* its image is then written out, giving

   THIRTYSEVEN

as the final result of the program.

8.3   Floating point subtypes

As we have seen, floating point values are held in a computer only as approximations and Ada has features which allow a programmer to specify their relative accuracy. In this way it should be possible to write programs in which the precision with which the values are held is specified by the program rather than by the computer hardware being used. This is important in areas such as numerical analysis and should lead to programs which are machine-independent. Details of this are beyond the scope of this book, but an idea of what is involved can be gathered from the following declarations.

   The subtype declaration

   subtype *short* **is** *real* **digits** 6;

means that any variable of this subtype must be stored with an accuracy of at least six significant decimal digits. A range constraint can also be given:

   subtype *probability* **is** *real* **range** 0.0 .. 1.0;

Both constraints can be applied in one declaration, with the accuracy constraint being given first.

   subtype *short_probability* **is** *real* **digits** 4 **range** 0.0 .. 1.0;

Of the various floating point attributes, *small* and *large* are of interest. The attribute *small* gives the smallest positive non-zero number which can be represented exactly, while the attribute *large* gives the largest number which can be represented exactly. The *digits* attribute gives the number of decimal digits of precision. Hence the attribute *float'digits* is implementation-dependent.

Exercises

1. Consider the following declarations:

   type *card* **is** (*two, three, four, five, six, seven, eight, nine, ten,*
               jack, queen, king, ace);
   subtype *face_card* **is** *card* **range** *jack* .. *king*;
   value : *card*;
   high_value : *face_card*;

   What values are assigned to the variables *value* and *high_value*
   in the following statements and which statements, if any,
   would cause *constraint_error* exceptions to be raised?

   value := *card'succ*(*three*);
   value := *face_card'pred*(*five*);
   high_value := *face_card'succ*(*face_card'first*);
   high_value := *card'pred*(*card'last*);
   value := *face_card'first*;
   value := *face_card'val*(0);

2. Declare each of the following subtypes:

   (a) A floating point subtype in which the values are held to an
   accuracy of six decimal digits and are in the range − 1.0 to
   + 1.0
   (b) A *card* subtype in which the values are lower than *eight*
   (c) An integer subtype in which all the values are less than zero

3. If we have the declaration

   subtype *lower_case* **is** *character* **range** 'a' .. 'z';

   what would be the effect of executing the following
   statements?

   for *ch* **in** 'a' .. 'z' **loop**
     put(*ch*);
   end loop;
   new_line;
   for *ch* **in** *lower_case'first* .. *lower_case'last* **loop**
     put(*ch*);
   end loop;
   new_line;
   for *ch* **in reverse** *lower_case* **loop**
     put(*ch*);
   end loop;

4. Using the information given in appendix 3, declare a subtype
   called *printable_character* whose values are the printable
   ASCII characters.

9

Arrays

9.1 Introduction

Let us consider the following problem. We have a group of 100 people, each of whose ages is known. We want to know their average age and how many of them are older than this.

We can find the average age easily enough by reading the 100 ages, adding them together and dividing the result by 100. To find the number of people of above average age requires us to look once again at the 100 individual ages. For the ages to be available for re-examination means that we have to store them somewhere.

This is a common problem in programming. We want to be able to store a large amount of information and be able to deal with it in a systematic manner. In such cases we use arrays.

An array is a composite object and consists of components each of which must have the same type or subtype. To help solve our problem, we could define the following array type

type *ages* **is array** (1 .. 100) **of** *natural*;

and then declare a variable of this type.

how_old : *ages*;

This declares a composite object called *how_old*, which consists of 100 components with each component being of subtype *natural*.

Individual components of the array are referred to by what is called an "index" or "subscript", which is written in brackets after the array variable name. The ages of the first three people in our list are therefore referred to as

how_old(1)   *how_old*(2)   *how_old*(3)

As you might expect, we must not use an index whose value is outside the range 1 to 100. If we try to do so a *constraint_error* exception will be raised.

A component of the array can be used anywhere an ordinary variable of subtype *natural* can be used. Hence we can have statements such as

> *how_old*(1) := 17;
> *how_old*(7) := *how_old*(1) + 5;
> *get*(*how_old*(4));
> *put*(*how_old*(4));

The value of the index determines which component is being used. After execution of these statements the first component of our array will have the value 17 and the seventh component the value 22.

The big advantage of using arrays is that the index can be an expression. This means that if we wish to perform the same calculations on each of the 100 ages, we can use a loop with the array index changing each time round the loop.

To show how this can be done, a solution to our ages problem is given in the following program. The average age is calculated to be a whole number, as that seems reasonable for this particular problem.

PROGRAM 9.1

```
with student_io; use student_io;
procedure older is
    sample_size : constant integer := 100;
    type ages is array (1 .. sample_size) of natural;
    how_old : ages;
    average : natural;
    sum_ages, number_older : natural := 0;
begin
    --read ages and calculate their average
    for person in 1 .. sample_size loop
      get(how_old(person));
      sum_ages := sum_ages + how_old (person);
    end loop;
    average := sum_ages / sample_size;
    --count the number older than average
    for person in 1 .. sample_size loop
      if how_old(person) > average then
        number_older := number_older + 1;
      end if;
    end loop;
    put("Average age is "); put(average, width => 1);
    new_line;
    put("Number older than average is ");
```

```
        put(number_older, width = > 1);
        new_line;
    end older;
```

In the first loop the 100 ages are read into the array and their sum is calculated. In the second loop the 100 ages stored in the array are compared in turn with the average and the number above average are counted. A constant identifier is used in the program instead of the integer literal 100 so that the program can easily be modified to deal with a group of a different size.

In the declaration of an array type there is no restriction on the type or subtype of the components. We can have arrays of real values, integers or of any enumeration type although, of course, the normal strict type-checking rules apply when they are used. The index is restricted to any discrete type or subtype.

The following examples give some more information about array declarations. If we wanted to hold the contents of a line of text and we knew that no line contained more than 80 characters, a suitable array type declaration would be

type *line* **is array** (1 .. 80) **of** *character*;

If we wished to hold the number of visitors' tickets sold at some ancient monument on each day of a week and our earlier definition of type *day* was available, we could have the declarations

type *daily_number* **is array** (*sun .. sat*) **of** *natural*;
ticket_number : *daily_number*;

The array *ticket_number* has seven components. Each component is of subtype *natural* and is identified by an index of type *day*. The following code could be used to read and store the information about the number of tickets sold on each day:

for *today* **in** *sun .. sat* **loop**
    get(ticket_number(today));
end loop;

Data for this would be seven positive whole numbers. You will find that for loops are often used when we are processing the contents of an array, as they give a convenient way of dealing with each component in turn.

A type mark can be used to indicate the index range in the definition of an array. The declaration

type *daily_number* **is array** (*day*) **of** *natural*;

is an alternative way of declaring the above array type, as too is

> **type** *daily_number* **is array** (*day* **range** *sun* .. *sat*) **of** *natural*;

Instead of declaring an array type and then declaring a variable of that type, it is possible to amalgamate the two declarations. We could, for example, have had

> *ticket_number* : **array** (*sun* .. *sat*) **of** *natural*;

In this case we have an anonymous array type. Such arrays cannot be used as procedure parameters because they have no name.

9.2 Two-dimensional arrays

The arrays described in the previous section are called one-dimensional arrays because the components are accessed using a single index. Multi-dimensional arrays are allowed in Ada, although arrays with more than two dimensions are seldom used. Two-dimensional arrays are a convenient way of holding tables of information.

Let us now look at how we can represent the 8×8 board for a chess-playing program. We first declare an enumeration type for the different kinds of chess pieces,

> **type** *piece* **is** (*blank*, *w_pawn*, *b_pawn*, *w_knight*, *b_knight*,
> *w_bishop*, *b_bishop*, *w_rook*, *b_rook*, *w_queen*,
> *b_queen*, *w_king*, *b_king*);

and then declare a two-dimensional array type and an object of this type,

> **type** *board* **is array** (1 .. 8, 1 .. 8) **of** *piece*;
> *chessboard* : *board*;

In the declaration we must give the range of possible index values for both dimensions. In this case both subscripts are to be in the range one to eight and so *chessboard* is an array with 64 components organized as eight rows and eight columns. Each component can take one of the 13 values of type *piece*.

The components are identified by two index values of type *integer*. Hence the statement

> *chessboard*(3, 4) := *w_pawn*;

causes the component at position row 3, column 4 to be given the value *w_pawn*.

Calculations involving the components of a two-dimensional array often use two nested for loops. If we assume that the chessboard has already been given suitable values, the following statements will calculate how many white pawns are left. The declaration

> *w_pawn_count* : *natural* := 0;

is assumed.

```
for row in 1 .. 8 loop
  for column in 1 .. 8 loop
    if chessboard(row, column) = w_pawn then
      w_pawn_count := w_pawn_count + 1;
    end if;
  end loop;
end loop;
```

We have seen how the numbers of tickets sold on each of seven days can be held in an array. The following array could be used if information about a four-week period was to be stored:

```
type month is array (1 .. 4, day) of natural;
tickets : month;
```

The first index is of type *integer* and the second is of type *day*. The following loop could be used to read 28 values into this array.

```
for week in 1 .. 4 loop
  for days in day loop
    get(tickets(week, days));
  end loop;
end loop;
```

Let us now consider the problem of reading the daily number of tickets sold in a four-week period and finding which of the seven days in the week is, on average, the most popular. That day should be printed out along with the numbers of tickets sold on it.

Our outline algorithm might be along the following lines:

> Read and store the number of tickets sold for each of the 28 days
>
> Calculate and store the total number of tickets sold on each day of the week
>
> Find the most popular day in the week
>
> Write result
>
> Write the four values making up the most popular choice

Before we develop the algorithm any further we must consider how we are going to store the required information. In general, when we solve problems on a computer we need not only to design algorithms, but also to decide on the appropriate "data structures".

In this case, as well as holding all 28 daily ticket numbers we may wish to store the seven sub-totals so that we can easily find which day is on average the most popular. This suggests that two arrays are required, a two-dimensional array to hold the 28 ticket numbers and a one-dimensional array to hold the seven sub-totals.

Once we have decided on the form of our data structures implementing the solution is relatively straightforward. The sub-totals can be calculated while the ticket numbers are being read in.

PROGRAM 9.2

```
with student_io; use student_io;
procedure popular is
   subtype week_range is positive range 1 .. 4;
   type day is (sunday, monday, tuesday, wednesday, thursday,
               friday, saturday);
   type month is array (week_range, day) of natural;
   type sub_total is array (day) of natural;
   tickets : month;
   day_total : sub_total;
   best_day : day := sunday;
   best_total : natural := 0;
begin
   --Read the number of tickets sold in a 28-day period
   --and calculate which day in the week is, on average,
   --the most popular
   for days in day loop
      day_total(days) := 0;
   end loop;
   --Read data and calculate the sub-totals
   for week in week_range loop
      for days in day loop
         get(tickets(week, days));
         day_total(days) := day_total(days) + tickets(week, days);
      end loop;
   end loop;
   --Find the most popular day in the week
   for days in day loop
      if day_total(days) > best_total then
         best_day := days;
         best_total := day_total(days);
      end if;
   end loop;
   put("On average the most popular day is ");
   put_line(day'image(best_day));
   --Write values making up the most popular day
```

```
put_line("The four components are");
for week in week_range loop
  put(tickets(week, best_day));
end loop;
new_line;
end popular;
```

Let us now trace the execution of the program. In the first loop the seven components of *day_total* are initialised to zero. The nested for loop is then entered. Each time round the inner loop, a number is read in, stored in the two-dimensional array and then added to the appropriate sub-total for that day of the week.

We then go on to find which day is on average the most popular by the usual technique of having a loop and each time round finding the "most popular so far". In the final loop the four components making up the best day are written out. Possible output from the program might be

On average the most popular day is SATURDAY

The four components are

    1342   1287   1176   984

9.3 Array type definition and array attributes

Now that we have seen how arrays can be declared and used, let us look at the details. The syntax diagram for an array type declaration is

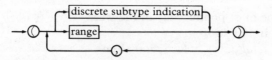

The array type definitions which we have been using have the form

→(array)→[index constraint]→(of)→[subtype indication]→

where an index constraint is defined by

If we assume the subtype declaration

subtype *letter* **is** *character* **range** 'a' .. 'z';

the following four array definitions are equivalent ways of defining an array with 26 integer components and with an index in the range 'a' to 'z':

array (*character* **range** 'a' .. 'z') **of** *integer*;
array ('a' .. 'z') **of** *integer*;
array (*letter*) **of** *integer*;
array (*letter* **range** 'a' .. 'z') **of** *integer*;

Several array attributes are defined and are best seen through an example. If we have the declarations

type *table* **is array** (1 .. 3, 0 .. 7) **of** *real*;
results : *table*;

then the following attributes are available:

(i) *table'first* and *results'first* give the lower bound of the first index range. This is the value 1.

(ii) *table'last* and *results'last* give the upper bound of the first index range. This is the value 3.

(iii) *table'first*(2), *results'first*(2), *table'last*(2) and *results'last*(2) give respectively the lower and upper bounds of the second index range. These are the values 0 and 7.

(iv) *table'range* and *results'range* give the first index range. This is the range 1 .. 3.

(v) *table'range*(2) and *results'range*(2) give the second index range. This is the range 0 .. 7.

(vi) *table'length* and *results'length* give the number of values in the first index range. This is the value 3.

(vii) *table'length*(2) and *results'length*(2) give the number of values in the second index range. This is the value 8.

With each of the attributes the first index range can also be indicated by having the value 1 in brackets after the attribute name. Hence *table'first*(1) is equivalent to *table'first*.

The value of one array can be assigned to another array and two arrays can be compared for equality or inequality with strict type checking being enforced as usual. Hence if we have the declarations

type *list* **is array** (1 .. 10) **of** *real*;
a, b : *list*;
c : **array** (1 .. 10) **of** *real*;

the assignment

$a := b$;

will cause each component of b to be assigned to the equivalent component of a. The expressions $a = b$ and $a /= b$ involve comparison of all the equivalent components in the two arrays. The array c, on the other hand, is regarded as a different type from either a or b even though it is structurally the same. Similarly

    type *another_list* **is array** (1 .. 10) **of** *real*;
    d : *another_list*;

declares an array which is of a different type from either of the previous ones. The rule about when two objects have the same type is sometimes called "name equivalence", i.e. they must have the same name for their base type.

Assignments of the form

    a(1) := *c*(1);

are still allowed because in this case both objects are of type *real*.

9.4　Arrays as parameters

Complete arrays can be passed as parameters to procedures and functions in the same way as scalar objects. The calculation of the most popular day in the week made in Program 9.2 could, for example, be replaced by a function declaration and an associated function call:

```
function best (totals : in sub_total) return day is
    popular_day : day := sunday;
    largest_total : natural := 0;
begin
    --find the position of the largest value in the array
    for which_day in totals'range loop
        if totals(which_day) > largest_total then
            popular_day := which_day;
            largest_total := totals (which_day);
        end if;
    end loop;
    return popular_day;
end best;
```

The associated function call would be

    best_day := *best*(*day_total*);

Because it is being passed to a function the array must be an **in** mode parameter. This is what we want, for we wish only to examine the contents of the array, not to change them. The type of the actual array parameter in the function call must be the same as the type of the formal parameter in the function declaration. They are both of type *sub_total*.

One operation which frequently occurs as part of the solution to a larger problem is sorting a list of objects into order. There are many different sort algorithms. If we have a short list of objects a method such as simple selection shown below is adequate, but for longer lists a more efficient method should be used. The principle behind simple selection sort is that it uses a loop which has the loop invariant that after the kth cycle the first k components in the list are in their final position. The value of k is in the range zero up to the length of the list.

Procedure *selection_sort* is passed a one-dimensional array of type *list* and it sorts it into non-decreasing order before passing it back to the calling routine. The mode of the list parameter must therefore be **in out**.

In the procedure we assume that a declaration such as

    type *list* **is array** (1 .. 15) **of** *integer*;

has already been made and that the components of the array have been given values before the procedure is entered.

```
procedure selection_sort(item : in out list) is
    small_pos : natural range list'range;
    smallest : integer;
begin
    --sort the components of the item list
    for low in list'first .. list'last - 1 loop
        --components in positions list'first to low - 1 are
        --now in their final positions
        --find the smallest remaining component
        small_pos := low; smallest := item(low);
        for pos in low + 1 .. list'last loop
            if smallest > item(pos) then
                small_pos := pos; smallest := item(pos);
            end if;
        end loop;
        --swap smallest with the item in position low
        item(small_pos) := item(low);
        item(low) := smallest;
        --components in position list'first to low are
        --now in their final positions
    end loop;
    --components in positions list'first to list'last - 1
    --are now in their final positions
    --the last component must therefore be in its final position
    --all components are in their final sorted positions
end selection_sort;
```

Selection sort works by going through the list and selecting the smallest element. This is swapped with the element at the beginning of the list. The smallest element is now in its final position and the remainder of the list is searched for the next smallest element which is swapped with the element in the second position in the list. The two smallest components are now in their final position. This process of cycling round the outer loop in the procedure and each time moving one more component into its final sorted position is continued until all the components have been moved to their correct positions.

Note that in the procedure array attributes are used to control the number of times the loops are executed. The procedure would therefore not need to be modified if the index bounds of type *list* were changed. Also note that, although the example deals with a list of integers, if we wished instead to deal with a list of any other type only the declarations would have to be changed. The actual instructions do not depend on the type of the array component.

9.5 Array aggregates

Scalar objects can be initialised when they are declared and so it is reasonable to ask if this is possible with array objects. Because an array is a composite type, the value of an array object consists of the values of all its components. This can be represented by what is known as an array aggregate.

The rules governing array aggregates are complicated and we shall not consider all possible situations. The simplest case is known as positional association, in which each component value is listed separately. In the example

> **type** *list* **is array** (1 .. 7) **of** *natural*;
> *different* : *list* := (5, 10, 15, 20, 25, 30, 35);

we have a list with seven components. The aggregate in the initialisation of list *different* consists of seven expressions separated by commas and surrounded by brackets. The value of the first expression in the aggregate is assigned to the first component of *different*, the value of the second expression to the second component and so on. Hence *different*(1) becomes equal to 5, *different*(2) to 10, etc.

If all components of the array are to be given the same value we use what is known as named association. Within the brackets of the aggregate the complete range of possible index values is given, followed first by " = > " and then by the value which is to be assigned to the components. An example of this is

> *same* : *list* := (1 .. 7 = > 1);

where all the components of *same* are initialised to one. An alternative, perhaps better, way of doing this would have been the declaration

same : *list* : = (*list'range* = > 1);

When an aggregate is used to give an array a value it must give a value to every component of the array; using the range attribute reduces the likelihood of error, especially if the bounds of the array were to be changed in some future modification of the program.

Named association can be used in more complicated situations. If, for example, we wanted a list where the first and third components were to be set to zero, the second and fourth to one and the remaining three components to two, we could write

another : *list* : = (1 | 3 = > 0, 2 | 4 = > 1, 5 .. 7 = > 2);

The symbol "|" is used to separate the index choices in a similar way to its use in the case statement.

An aggregate could have been used in the declaration of *day_total* in Program 9.2 to initialise all its components to zero. The first loop in the program would not then have been necessary. The aggregate could have been given in several different ways, such as

day_total : *sub_total* : = (0, 0, 0, 0, 0, 0, 0);
day_total : *sub_total* : = (*sub_total'range* = > 0);
day_total : *sub_total* : = (*sunday* .. *saturday* = > 0);
day_total : *sub_total* : = (*day* = > 0);

These declarations would all have the same effect.

Multi-dimensional arrays can be given a value. If we have the type

type *table* **is array** (1 .. 2, 1 .. 5) **of** *real*;

then an array object can be initialised either as

results : *table* : = (1 .. 2 = > (1 .. 5 = > 0.0));

or as

results : *table* : = ((1 .. 5 = > 0.0), (1 .. 5 = > 0.0));

The aggregate is therefore written as a one-dimensional aggregate, each of whose values are themselves one-dimensional aggregates. This can be generalised to arrays of any dimension.

Finally, if we know that the value of an array is not going to be changed once it has been initialised it can be declared as a constant object, as in

fives : **constant** *list* : = (5, 10, 15, 20, 25, 30, 35);

A constant array must be given a value when it is declared.

Exercises

1. Trace the execution of the following program using a data value of your choice:

   with *student_io*; **use** *student_io*;
   procedure *search* **is**
     type *vals* **is array**(0 .. 8) **of** *integer*;
     value_list : *vals* := (0, 7, 17, 5, 29, 13, 19, 3, 11);
     position : *natural* := 8;
     number : *integer*;
   begin
     get(*number*);
     value_list(0) := *number*;
     while *value_list*(*position*) /= *number* **loop**
       position := *position* − 1;
     end loop;
     if *position* > 0 **then**
       put("position is"); *put*(*position*);
       new_line;
     else
       put_line("number not in list");
     end if;
   end *search*;

2. We have an array declared as

   type *list* **is array** (1 .. 50) **of** *positive*;
   A : *list*;

   Write a sequence of statements which will read 50 positive integers into this array and then find the position in the array of the smallest.

3. Write a function which, when passed an array of type *list*, will return the position in the array of the smallest component.

4. Write a program to read in ten numbers and then write them out in reverse order.

5. (a) Declare an enumeration type *month* to represent the twelve months of the year.

   (b) Declare a 12-component array constant which will hold the number of days in each month of the current year.

   (c) Design a function which, when given a date, will return which day in the year it is. For example, given February 5 it will return the value 36.

6. (a) We have the subtype declarations

   subtype *lower_case* **is** *character* **range** 'a' .. 'z';
   subtype *upper_case* **is** *character* **range** 'A' .. 'Z';

   Declare a 26-component array whose components are of type *upper_case* and whose index values are of type *lower_case*. Assign values to each component of the array so that each component has the value which is the upper case counterpart of its index.

   (b) Write a procedure which will read a line of text consisting of upper and lower case letters and punctuation characters, and write it out in a form where all the lower case letters have been converted to upper case.

10

Unconstrained Arrays

10.1 Introduction

Let us again consider the procedure whereby a list of 15 numbers were sorted into non-decreasing order. A drawback of this procedure is that it only works for an array with 15 components. Does this mean that we need to write a separate procedure for each different size of list?

The answer to that question is no. The arrays we have looked at up till now have been defined by what is called a "constrained array definition". Ada also allows arrays to be defined by an "unconstrained array definition", where the bounds are not specified when the array type is declared. It is then possible for different arrays to have the same base type although they have different index bounds. The type of the index values, the type of the components and the number of dimensions are the same for the different arrays; it is only the size of the array which may differ.

As an example of this let us look at how we can go about producing a procedure which will be capable of sorting any one-dimensional array which has integer components and index values which are natural numbers. We must first declare an array type which has an unconstrained array definition:

type *any_list* **is array** (*natural* **range** < >) **of** *integer*;

Here we have declared an array type called *any_list* which has one dimension, has components of type *integer* and whose index values are of subtype *natural*. The index range is undefined and is represented by " < > ", which we refer to as a box.

We can now declare array objects of this array type, but in the declaration of an array object an index constraint must be given to specify the index bounds, as in

numbers : *any_list*(1 .. 15);
more_numbers : *any_list*(0 .. 20);

Here two array objects have been declared. They are both of type *any_ list*, but *numbers* has 15 components while *more_numbers* has 21 components. We have one array type, but two different array subtypes.

We now want to be able to declare a procedure which, assuming that values have been assigned to both the arrays *numbers* and *more_ numbers*, will allow both the calls

> *selection_sort(numbers)*;
> *selection_sort(more_numbers)*;

We have, in fact, to make very few changes to our existing selection sort procedure because it does not explicitly mention the bounds of the array being sorted, but instead uses array attributes. There is, however, one major change. Our existing procedure uses the attributes of the array type. Although this is allowed with a constrained array type, we cannot refer to the attributes of an unconstrained array type because attributes such as *first*, *last*, etc. are not fixed. What we can do though is refer to the attributes of the array object because when the procedure is called they are fixed by the subtype of the actual array parameter. Our procedure therefore becomes

```
procedure selection_sort(item : in out any_list) is
   small_pos : natural range item'range;
   smallest : integer;
begin
   --sort the components of item
   for low in item'first .. item'last − 1 loop
      --components in positions item'first to low − 1 are
      --now in their final positions
      --find the smallest remaining component
      small_pos := low; smallest := item(low);
      for pos in low + 1 .. item'last loop
         if smallest > item(pos) then
            small_pos := pos; smallest := item(pos);
         end if;
      end loop;
      --swap smallest with the item in position low
      item(small_pos) := item(low);
      item(low) := smallest;
      --components in positions item'first to low are
      --now in their final positions
```

end loop;
--components in positions item'first to item'last − 1
--are now in their final positions
--the last component must therefore be in its final position
--all components are in their final sorted positions
end *selection_sort*;

When we have the procedure call

selection_sort(numbers);

the attributes *item'range*, *item'first* and *item'last* are the same as *numbers'range*, *numbers'first* and *numbers'last*. The procedure will therefore sort a list of 15 components. When the procedure call is

selection_sort(more_numbers);

the attributes are *more_numbers'range*, *more_numbers'first* and *more_numbers'last*, and so a list of 21 components is sorted.

Now that we have seen how they can be used, let us look at the syntax diagram for an unconstrained array definition. It is

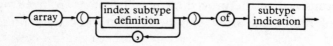

where an index subtype definition is defined by

It follows from this that if we have a two-dimensional array then both index ranges must be given, in which case we have a constrained array definition, or both must be left unspecified.

Many numerical analysis algorithms require information to be held in a two-dimensional array called a matrix. A declaration such as

type *matrix* **is array** (*positive* **range** < >,
            positive **range** < >) **of** *real*;

allows us to declare matrices which are of different sizes but have the same base type. This means that it is possible to write general matrix handling subprograms. Example of matrix objects would be

table : matrix(1 .. 6, 1 .. 4);
larger_table : matrix(1 .. 7, 1 .. 22);

Declarations of array objects can take place in two stages. We can first declare a subtype

subtype *list_of_ten* **is** *any_list*(1 .. 10);

and then declare an object of this subtype

>*answers* : *list_of_ten*;

This is useful when we wish to have several different array objects with the same bounds.

Composite values such as arrays can be returned by functions. As an example, consider the following function where the values of the corresponding components in two lists are added together:

```
function add_lists(list_a, list_b : any_list) return any_list is
    new_list : any_list(list_a'range);
begin
    --add components of two lists
    for pos in list_a'range loop
        new_list(pos) := list_a(pos) + list_b(pos);
    end loop;
    return new_list;
end add_lists;
```

The types of the two parameters and the returned value are unconstrained arrays. The bounds of the parameters are fixed by the bounds of the actual parameters used in the function call. The bounds of the returned array are fixed by the bounds of the array in the return statement.

Hence, if we had the declarations

>*first, second, sum* : *any_list*(1 .. 10);

and values had been assigned to the components of the first two arrays, the statement

>*sum* := *add_lists(first, second)*;

would give values to the components of sum such that

>*sum*(1) was equal to *first*(1) + *second*(1)
>*sum*(2) was equal to *first*(2) + *second*(2)
>   . . .
>*sum*(10) was equal to *first*(10) + *second*(10)

The two actual array parameters and the array to which the resulting value is assigned must, in this example, all have the same index bounds. If they do not a *constraint_error* exception will be raised.

Note that in the function the size of the local array object *new_list* is not known until the function is called. It has the same size as the first parameter in the call and so it can differ in size in different calls of the function. This is an example of what is called a dynamic array.

10.2 **Strings**

We have been using the built-in type *string* in most of our programs. As we have seen, string literals are written as a series of zero or more characters enclosed by quotation characters, as in

"This is a string literal"

A string is therefore a composite type whose components are characters. It is, in fact, a one-dimensional unconstrained array type which has been declared behind the scenes as

type *string* **is array** (*positive* **range** < >) **of** *character*;

This means that string variables and constants can be declared in the same way as any other array objects. Hence

line : *string*(1 .. 80);

declares a one-dimensional array object of type *string* which has 80 components of type *character*.

We have already come across the declaration of string constants such as

greeting : **constant** *string* := "Hello";

Note that an index constraint has not been given in this declaration; instead the bounds are deduced from the string literal. This is allowed only with array constants, not with array variables. A fuller definition would have been

greeting : **constant** *string*(1 .. 5) := "Hello";

Ordinary array aggregates can also be used in giving a string a value, as in

greeting : **constant** *string* := ('H', 'e', 'l', 'l', 'o');

Although in this case using the string literal is superior, aggregates are useful when all the components are to be given the same value. The declaration of border in Program 3.4 could, for example, be replaced by

border : **constant** *string* := (1 .. 25 => '*');

A string literal can be assigned to a string variable in an assignment statement, but the literal must contain the correct number of characters. Hence if we have the declaration

name : *string*(1 .. 10);

the name can only be assigned a ten character string literal, as in

name := "James   ";

The trailing spaces are necessary.

Because *name* is an array, individual components can be accessed in the normal way. The value of *name*(3) for example is the character 'm'.

Having to ensure that the correct number of trailing spaces has been included in a string literal can become rather annoying. Let us write a procedure to copy the contents of one string to another and, if the string being copied is too short, to pad it out with trailing spaces. If it is too long then only characters at the start of the string will be copied. So that the procedure can work with strings of any length, array attributes are used to control the loops.

```
procedure copy(old : in string; new_st : out string) is
    old_index : positive := old'first;
    new_index : positive := new_st'first;
begin
    --copy old string to new string
    loop
        --copy components until the end of one string is
        --encountered
        --test at beginning so that null strings are handled
        exit when new_index > new_st'last;
        if old_index > old'last then
            --pad new string with trailing blanks
            for pos in new_index .. new_st'last loop
                new_st(pos) := ' ';
            end loop;
            exit;
        end if;
        new_st(new_index) := old(old_index);
        new_index := new_index + 1;
        old_index := old_index + 1;
    end loop;
end copy;
```

A possible call of this procedure is

```
copy("James", name);
```

No trailing blanks are required.

A shorter form of the copy procedure can be produced by using what is known as a "slice". A slice is a sequence of consecutive components of a one-dimensional array. The slice

```
name (1 .. 3)
```

is the string "Jam", while the slice

```
name(2 .. 5)
```

is the string "ames". A slice of an array variable is itself an array variable. This allows assignments such as

name(2 .. 5) := "immy";

after which *name* will have the value "Jimmy   ".

Slices and an array aggregate are used in the following procedure to copy the string contents instead of them being copied character by character in a loop. In an array assignment the number of components in the array variable and in the array value must be the same or a *constraint_error* exception will be raised.

```
procedure copy(old : in string; new_st : out string) is
begin
    --copy old string to new string
    if new_st'length > old'length then
        --old'length characters copied from old string to new
        --and new string padded with trailing blanks
        new_st := (new_st'range => ' ');
        new_st(new_st'first .. new_st'first + old'length − 1)
            := old;
    else
        --new_st'length characters copied from old string to new
        new_st := old(old'first .. old'first + new_st'length − 1);
    end if;
end copy;
```

Strings may be compared using the relational operators "=", "/=", ">", ">=", "<" and "<=" even when they are of differing length, as we saw in chapter 4, although of course for two strings to be equal they must have the same length.

The type of an array component is not restricted to the scalar types; we can also have arrays of composite types such as arrays. A common use of this is arrays of strings. As an example consider a VDU screen which can hold 24 lines with each line containing up to 80 characters. This information could be held in an array called *screen*, declared as

subtype *line* **is** *string*(1 .. 80);
screen : **array** (1 .. 24) **of** *line*;

The value of *screen*(1) is a string of 80 characters and as this is of course itself an array we refer to a component such as the third character in the first line as *screen*(1)(3).

10.3 String processing

In this book we are learning to design and write programs for ourselves, but many computer users only use programs which have already been written by other people. It is important that these programs are straightforward to use and are self-explanatory. They often proceed by means of a series of questions and answers. Non-numerical answers are usually stored in a string.

A procedure called *get_line*, which we have not encountered before but which is defined in package *student_io*, is of help here. The effect of

    get_line(st, length);

where *st* is a string variable and *length* is of subtype *natural*, is to read a sequence of characters and to store them in string *st*. Reading stops when either the end of line or the end of the string is encountered. If the end of line is encountered, the line terminator is then skipped. The index position of the last character read is put in *length*. If the line being read is empty, no characters are read and *length* is set equal to *st'first* − 1. This procedure is used to read and store a line of text so that its contents can be examined.

When we write out the contents of such a line we do not want to write all the components of *st*, but only those in positions *st'first* to *length*. This can be achieved by using the slice

    st(st'first .. length)

This allows the following statements to be used to read and then write out a line of text:

    get_line(st, length);
    put_line(st(st'first .. length));

The following program shows a simple example of a question and answer session. It uses the catenate operator which was introduced in chapter 3.

PROGRAM 10.1

```
with student_io; use student_io;
procedure questions is
   subtype line is string(1 .. 80);
   name, answer : line;
   name_length, answer_length : natural := 0;
begin
   --capital question program
   put_line("Hello, what is your name?");
   get_line(name, name_length);
   put_line("Hello, " & name(1 .. name_length));
   put_line("Would you like to answer a question?");
   loop
      get_line(answer, answer_length);
```

```
        if answer(1 .. answer_length) = "yes" then
          put_line("What is the capital of the United States?");
          get_line(answer, answer_length);
          if answer(1 .. answer_length) = "Washington" then
            put_line("Well done, " & name( 1 .. name_length)
                     & ", that is correct.");
            exit;
          else
            put_line("Sorry, " & name(1 .. name_length)
                     & ", that is wrong.");
            put_line("Would you like to try again?");
          end if;
        elsif answer(1 .. answer_length) = "no" then
          exit;
        else
          put_line("Please type either yes or no.");
        end if;
      end loop;
      put_line("Bye, " & name(1 .. name_length));
    end questions;
```

This program has made extensive use of slices and strings, but you should have no trouble in following it. A possible dialogue might be

```
Hello, what is your name?
John
Hello, John
Would you like to answer a question?
OK
Please type either yes or no.
yes
What is the capital of the United States?
New York
Sorry, John, that is wrong.
Would you like to try again?
yes
What is the capital of the United States?
Washington
Well done, John, that is correct.
Bye, John
```

10.4   Example problem

To give us further practice in representing and manipulating strings, let us now consider a more complicated problem. We are to read lines of text and find out on which lines, if any, the following words appear:

begin   else   end   for   if   loop   then   while

The words may appear in either upper or lower case and we may assume that no line contains more than 80 characters. The text is to be terminated by a full stop typed alone at the beginning of a line.

A possible outline algorithm is

```
loop
    read and store the next line of text
    leave loop if the terminating line has been read
    loop while still more characters in the line
        take next word
        if the word is in the list then
            store details
        end if
    end loop
    write information about the words on the current line
end loop
```

Our next step must be to think about the data structures which we are to use. A string of 80 characters would seem to be the obvious method of holding the line under consideration. The eight special words whose occurrences are to be noted must be held somewhere so that each word in the text can be compared with them. A possible approach would be to hold the special words in a list and then check each word in the text against this list.

Before we go on to implement the design, we must consider what we mean by a "word". Let us take it to be a sequence of letters terminated by some character other than a letter.

We now come to the implementation. If the eight special words are to be held in a list and this list is not going to be changed during execution of the program, a constant array of strings would seem to be appropriate. As the maximum size of a special word is five characters, this can be declared as

```
subtype word is string(1 .. 5);
type special_list is array (positive range < >) of word;
word_list : constant special_list := ("begin", "else", "end ",
                    "for ", "if  ", "loop ", "then ", "while");
```

Each of the strings in the array aggregate must have five characters and so the trailing blanks are necessary.

A complete listing of the program to solve the problem is now given:

PROGRAM 10.2

```
with student_io; use student_io;
procedure find_words is
  line : string(1 .. 80);
  line_length : natural range 0 .. line'last := 0;
  char_no : natural range 0 .. line'last + 1 := 0;
  --char_no is the current position in the line
  subtype word is string(1 .. 5);
  next_word : word;
  type special_list is array (positive range <>) of word;
  word_list : constant special_list := ("begin", "else", "end  ",
                      "for ", "if ", "loop ", "then ", "while");
  word_found : Boolean := false;

function letter(ch : character) return Boolean is
begin
  --determine if the character is a letter
  return ch in 'a' .. 'z' or ch in 'A' .. 'Z';
end letter;

function lower_case(ch : character) return character is
begin
  --convert upper case letters to lower case
  if ch in 'A' .. 'Z' then
    return character'val(character'pos(ch) + character'pos('a')
        - character'pos('A'));
  else
    return ch;
  end if;
end lower_case;

procedure get_word(curr_line : string; ch_pos : in out natural;
                   length : positive; the_word : out word) is
  pos : positive := 1;
begin
  --get next word from curr_line starting at ch_pos + 1
  --find start of next word
  loop
    ch_pos := ch_pos + 1;
    exit when ch_pos = length or letter(curr_line(ch_pos));
  end loop;
  --scan the next word
  --remember words with < 6 characters
  the_word := "     ";
  while ch_pos <= length and then letter(curr_line(ch_pos))
  loop
```

```
      if pos < = 5 then
        the_word(pos) := lower_case(curr_line(ch_pos));
      elsif pos = 6 then
        --word too long, reset the_word
        the_word := "      ";
      end if;
      ch_pos := ch_pos + 1; pos := pos + 1;
    end loop;
end get_word;

function in_list(new_word : word) return Boolean is
begin
    --find if the word is in the list
    for pos in word_list'range loop
      --note multiple exit from loop
      if new_word = word_list(pos) then
        return true;
      end if;
    end loop;
    return false;
end in_list;

begin --Main Program
    --program to find occurrences of certain words in a text
    loop
      --read the next line
      get_line(line, line_length);
      exit when line_length = 1 and then line(1) = '.';
      char_no := 0; word_found := false;
      --take each word and check it against the list
      while char_no < line_length loop
        get_word(line, char_no, line_length, next_word);
        --find if the word is in the list
        if in_list(next_word) then
          put_line(next_word);
          word_found := true;
        end if;
      end loop;
      if word_found then
        put_line("found in");
        put_line(line(1 .. line_length));
      end if;
    end loop;
end find_words;
```

If this program was presented with the line

if ch in 'A' .. 'Z' then

the result would be

if
then
found in
if ch in 'A' .. 'Z' then

Two statements in the program are worth special mention. In procedure *get_word* the while loop is controlled by the Boolean expression

$ch\_pos <\ =$ *length* **and then** *letter(curr_line(ch_pos))*

Because it is possible for *ch_pos* to become greater than *length*, the short-circuit control form **and then** is necessary to protect against evaluation of *curr_line(ch_pos)* when *ch_pos* is greater than 80. That would lead to a *constraint_error* exception being raised.

The short-circuit control form in

line_length = 1 **and then** *line*(1) = '.'

not only stops unnecessary evaluation of the second relational expression when *line_length* is not equal to 1, but, when the first line is blank, it also stops examination of *line*(1) when it is still undefined.

Exercises

1. We have a type *list* declared as

   type *list* **is array**(*integer* **range** < >) **of** *positive*;

   Design a procedure which will be able to write out the components of any array that has been declared to be of this type. One of the parameters of the procedure should indicate how many components are to be written on each line, with the default being one component per line.

2. We have the declarations

   name : *string*(1 .. 15) := "Pascal programs";
   new_name : *string*(1 .. 12);

   What will be the value of *new_name* after the following slice assignments have taken place?

   new_name(1 .. 3) := "Ada";
   new_name(4 .. 12) := *name*(7 .. 15);

3. Procedure *get_line* is described in section 10.3. Let us assume

that this procedure was not available, but we would like it to
be. Design such a procedure.

4. What would be the effect of executing the following program?

```
with student_io; use student_io;
procedure join is
    st : string(1 .. 50);
    length : natural := 0;

    procedure append(stem : in out string; suffix : in string;
                     stem_length : in out natural) is
        start : positive := stem_length + 1;
    begin
        if stem_length + suffix'length < = stem'last then
            stem_length := stem_length + suffix'length;
            stem(start .. stem_length) := suffix;
        end if;
    end append;

begin
    st(1 .. 6) := "return";
    put_line(st(1 .. 6) & "ing");
    length := 6;
    append(st, "ing", length);
    put_line(st(1 .. length));
end join;
```

5. We have stored in a program, as an array of strings, the names
of 100 people. No name consists of more than 20 characters
and shorter names are padded with trailing blanks. What type
and object declarations will be required to hold this
information?

Modify procedure *selection_sort* in section 10.1 so that it will
be capable of sorting the 100 names into alphabetic order.

11

Records

11.1 Introduction

Arrays are composite types that have two important features. First, all components of an array are of the same type; secondly, array components have a computable index. This means they can be used in situations such as a loop, with a different component being accessed each time round the loop. There are, however, situations where arrays are not the best way of holding a collection of values.

Quite often in a program we have several pieces of information which are always used together. To represent a date for example, we need the day, month and year. We could use three different variables for this, but it would not then be clear that the three pieces of information are logically connected. Because they do not have the same type we cannot use an array, but even if they all had the same type, an array with three components would not be a particularly meaningful way of representing the information.

What we need is a composite type where the components can have different types and where individual components can be selected in a meaningful way. In Ada, such a composite type is called a record.

A date record type can be declared as

    type *which_month* **is** (*Jan, Feb, March, April, May, June,*
                                July, Aug, Sep, Oct, Nov, Dec);

    type *date* **is**
    record
        day : *positive* **range** 1 .. 31;
        month : *which_month*;
        year : *positive* **range** 1900 .. 1999;
    end record;

Variables of type *date*, such as

    birthday, day_after : *date*;

each have three components which are written as

    birthday.day   *birthday.month*   *birthday.year*

Record components can be used anywhere we can use simple variables, subject to the usual type-checking rules. The following assignment statements are therefore possible:

```
birthday.day := 15;
birthday.month := Sep;
birthday.year := 1944;
day_after.day := birthday.day + 1;
```

It is also possible to assign the value of one record to another record of the same type and to compare two records for equality or inequality.

Record aggregates are also available. The components can either be given by position or they can be specified by name. Hence the assignments

```
birthday := (15, Sep, 1944);
birthday := (day => 15, month => Sep, year => 1944);
```

are alternative ways of giving *birthday* the same value as the three separate assignment statements given above.

When constant records are declared they must be given a value, as in

```
last_day : constant date := (31, Dec, 1999);
```

Complete records can be passed as parameters to a subprogram or returned as values of a function. As an example, the following function takes one date and returns the date of the next day:

```
function next_day(today : date) return date is
   next : date := today;
begin
   --find and return the date following today
   case today.month is
      when April | June | Sep | Nov =>
         if today.day = 30 then
            next.day := 1;
            next.month := which_month'succ(today.month);
         else
            next.day := today.day + 1;
         end if;
      when Dec =>
         if today.day = 31 then
```

```
        next := (1, Jan, today.year + 1);
      else
        next.day := today.day + 1;
      end if;
    when Feb = >
      if (today.year rem 4 = 0 and today.day = 29) or
        (today.year rem 4 /= 0 and today.day = 28) then
        next.day := 1;
        next.month := March;
      else
        next.day := today.day + 1;
      end if;
    when Jan | March | May | July | Aug |Oct = >
      if today.day = 31 then
        next.day := 1;
        next.month := which_month'succ(today.month);
      else
        next.day := today.day + 1;
      end if;
    end case;
    return next;
  end next_day;
```

11.2 Composite components

As you might expect, the components of a record can themselves be composite objects such as arrays or records, and it is also
possible to have arrays of records.

This is shown in the following example, where we wish to hold
information about book loans in a small library. Each book is identified by an eight-character code and each library member by a six-
digit number. We want to hold this information about each book on
loan together with the date when it is due to be returned and a flag to
indicate whether or not the book is overdue.

If we assume that no more than 500 books can be on loan at any one
time, the information could be held in an array of records declared as

```
    type book is
    record
      code : string(1 .. 8);
      reader_num : positive range 100000 .. 999999;
      due : date;
      overdue : Boolean := false;
```

end record;
loan : **array** (1 .. 500) **of** *book*;

Record components can be given a default initial value. In this case each *overdue* component is initially set at *false*. Once the information about borrowed books has been recorded in the array, the following code could be used to write out the reader numbers and book codes for each overdue book.

```
for i in loan'range loop
   if loan(i).overdue then
      put(loan(i).code);
      put(loan(i).reader_num);
      new_line;
   end if;
end loop;
```

Each component of the array such as *loan*(5) is a record of type *book*. The components of this record are therefore written as

loan(5).*code* *loan*(5).*reader_num* *loan*(5).*due* *loan*(5).*overdue*

The type of these components are *string*, *integer*, *date* and *Boolean* respectively.

Because the *due* component of *book* is itself a record (of type *date*), we refer to its components individually as

loan(5).*due.day* *loan*(5).*due.month* *loan*(5).*due.year*

Similarly, because a string is an array of characters, components such as the fourth character of the book code are written as

loan(5).*code*(4)

The notation might seem strange at first, but it is straightforward and you should quickly become used to it.

More complicated record types are possible, but are not dealt with here. We have restricted ourselves to record type definitions which have the form

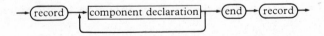

where a component declaration is defined as

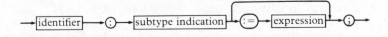

New record types must always be given a name in a type declaration; we cannot declare objects of an anonymous record type as we can with arrays.

11.3 A stack example

As another example of a record, let us consider the implementation of a stack. A stack is a list in which new items can be added and existing items removed at only one end. The last item on is therefore the first item to be removed. We refer to the end at which items can be added or removed as the "top of the stack".

Stacks are very important data structures in computer science and we shall discuss some of their uses later. They can be implemented in many different ways, although we always need a means of holding the items in the stack and a way of indicating the position of the current top item.

The type of the stack items does not affect the general principle. In the following discussion we assume that a type called *item* has already been declared and that we are implementing a stack of elements of type *item*. The declarations can easily be changed so that a stack of some other type such as *integer*, *character* or *date* is implemented.

The following declaration creates a stack type which can hold up to 100 items:

```
type item_list is array (positive range < >) of item;
type item_stack is
   record
      element : item_list(1 .. 100);
      top : natural := 0;
   end record;
```

The first component of the record is used to hold the stack elements and the second element is the stack pointer. The stack pointer always points to the item which is currently at the top of the stack. It is given a default initial value of zero to represent an empty stack.

Empty stacks can then be declared by object declarations such as

```
results, holding : item_stack;
```

The two principal stack operations are adding a new item to the top of a stack and removing the current top item from a stack. We say that we "push" an item on to a stack and "pop" an item from a stack.

Procedures to carry out these operations are

```
procedure push(x : item; stack : in out item_stack) is
begin
```

```
--add item to the stack
if stack.top = 100 then
    put_line("Stack is already full");
else
    stack.top := stack.top + 1;
    stack.element(stack.top) := x;
end if;
end push;
procedure pop(x : out item; stack : in out item_stack) is
begin
--remove top item from the stack
if stack.top = 0 then
    put_line("Stack is empty");
else
    x := stack.element(stack.top);
    stack.top := stack.top - 1;
end if;
end pop;
```

In each case we must check against attempting to add an item to a full stack or removing an item from an empty stack.

As a simple example of a stack operation, let us consider *this* and *that* to be two variables of type *item*. The effect of executing

> *push(this, results)*; *push(that, results)*;
> *pop(this, results)*; *pop(that, results)*;

is to swap the current values of *this* and *that*.

Exercises

1. Function *next_day* in section 11.1 will raise a *constraint_error* exception when asked to find the day following 31 Dec 1999. Change the function so that when this situation arises, it prints an error message and does not try to update the date.

2. Modify, and suitably rename, function *next_day* so that it returns the value of the preceding day.

3. Rational numbers can be represented as two integers, a numerator and a denominator. Construct a suitable type declaration for rational numbers and then write a function which will take as parameters two rational numbers and return their sum as a result.

4. We have the following declarations to represent a deck of cards:

```
type face_value is (none, two, three, four, five, six, seven,
                          eight, nine, ten, jack, queen, king, ace);
type suits is (empty, clubs, diamonds, hearts, spades);
type cards is record
              value : face_value;
              suit : suits;
            end record;
type hand is array(1 .. 13) of cards;
type deck is array(1 .. 52) of cards;
void : constant cards := (value => none, suit => empty);
```

In the games of whist and bridge the 52 cards in a deck are
dealt into four hands of 13 cards. Write code for each of the
following function and procedure skeletons:

```
procedure deal_cards(all_cards : deck;
                     north, east, south, west : out hand) is
begin
   --take a deck of cards and deal it into four hands
end deal_cards;
function aces_in_hand(dealt : hand) return natural is
begin
   --return the number of aces in the hand
end aces_in_hand;
function number(dealt : hand; which_one : face_value)
                     return natural is
begin
   --return the number of cards in the hand with the
   --face value of which_one
end number;
procedure low_heart(dealt: in out hand; played : out cards)
is
begin
   --the lowest heart in the hand is played and it is
   --then removed from the hand
   --if there are no hearts the value void is returned
   --as the value played
end low_heart;
```

5. Consider the following declarations:

```
type reply is
   record
      contents : string(1 .. 80);
```

```
    length : natural;
  end record;
procedure get_response(current : out reply) is
begin
    get_line(current.contents, current.length);
end get_response;
procedure put_response(current : reply) is
begin
    put(current.contents(1 .. current.length));
end put_response;
```

Rewrite Program 10.1 so that the person's name and the answers to the questions are held in objects of type *reply*. The reading and writing of responses should be done using the procedures *get_response* and *put_response* defined above. A function called *equal* should be written to check the replies. It should have one parameter of type *reply* and one of type *string*.

12

Packages

12.1 Solving large problems

Our approach to solving problems has been to divide the initial problem into a series of subproblems, each of which is more or less independent of the others. We have then progressed by attempting to solve each of the subproblems separately. This has usually involved dividing a subproblem into a series of yet simpler subproblems. The idea has been that once the solutions to all the subproblems have been obtained, they can be put together to give the solution to the overall problem. Even though our problems have all been fairly small, our central theme has been that problems are best solved by splitting them into a series of smaller problems.

The language tool which has helped us implement this strategy has been the subprogram. Our Ada programs have consisted of one main procedure within which we have declared other subprograms. The subprograms have often corresponded to statements in the top-level algorithm, and this has meant that the number of statements in the final main procedure has not been significantly larger than the number of statements in the top-level algorithm.

The advantage of subprograms is that they allow us to hide detail. Once a subprogram has been written and tested we are interested only in what it can do and how it can be called. The internal details of how it carries out the operation can be safely ignored. This is how we manage to master the complexity of a problem; we concentrate on one thing at a time and do not let ourselves be distracted by unnecessary detail.

The question which now arises is whether or not subprograms are going to be sufficiently good at hiding detail when we come to deal with larger problems.

Consider, for example, our string processing problem (Program 10.2). In this program we call procedure *get_line* to read a line of text and procedure *get_word* to get the next word from this line. The rest of the program does not need to know about the line, its length or the current position reached in scanning it. But because these variables are declared in the main procedure, they are visible throughout the program. This has two disadvantages. The main part of the program is cluttered with unwanted detail, and the variables are not protected from being changed inadvertently.

What we need is to be able to make information available to one or more subprograms and yet be hidden from the rest of the program. This requires a means of packaging together a group of logically related subprograms, types and objects. It must be possible to select which information is to be visible from outside the package and which information is to be hidden behind the package walls.

This extension to the subprogram concept gives us a powerful mechanism by which we can split large problems into self-contained units, each of which can be solved independently.

The package is the means by which this can be done in Ada. A package can be in two parts, the package specification whose contents may be seen by other parts of a program, and an optional package body whose contents are hidden. In this chapter we shall look at package specifications and how types and objects can be declared and made visible to other parts of the program. In the next chapter we shall look at the use of subprograms in packages and at package bodies.

12.2 Ada program structure

We have used the library package called *student_io* in all our programs. It was made available each time by putting the context clause

> **with** *student_io*; **use** *student_io*;

in front of the main procedure. This context clause consists of a with clause followed by a use clause. It is the with clause which makes the contents of the package available. If we missed out the use clause we could still refer to all the subprograms in *student_io*, but we would have to use the package name when referring to them, as in

> *student_io.new_line*;

> *student_io.put*("This could be shorter");

This has the advantage of making it clear where the subprograms were declared, but gets rather tedious. It is the use clause which allows abbreviated forms such as

> *new_line*;

> *put*("This is shorter");

As well as using the contents of existing library packages, we want to be able to declare new packages for ourselves. How can this be done?

Like a subprogram, a package can be declared within a main procedure, or indeed inside any subprogram or other package. But unlike a subprogram it is normally declared separately outside the main procedure, as part of what is known as a compilation unit. The usual form of compilation unit is a context clause together with a package or a main procedure. An Ada program consists of a series of compilation units, one of which must contain the main procedure.

12.3 Package specifications

Let us now look at package specifications through a simple example.

We have a lottery and ticket owners wish to find out if they have won a prize. The information about the winning numbers is to be held in a package and our main procedure will interrogate the package contents.

PROGRAM 12.1

```
package winning is
   type list is array (positive range < >) of natural;
   win_list : constant list := (2546, 3479, 4321, 5173,
                                9716, 9837);
end winning;

with student_io; use student_io;
with winning; use winning;
procedure look_up is
   --identifiers list and win_list declared in winning
   ticket_number : natural;

   function in_list(number : natural;
                    search_list : list) return Boolean is
   begin
      --find if number is in the list
      for pos in search_list'range loop
         --note multiple exit from loop
         if number = search_list(pos) then
            return true;
         end if;
      end loop;
      return false;
   end in_list;

begin
```

```
--read ticket number and check if it wins a prize
put("What is your number?");
get(ticket_number);
if in_list(ticket_number, win_list) then
    put_line("Well done, you have won a prize");
else
    put_line("Sorry, better luck next time");
end if;
end look_up;
```

Package *winning* contains a type declaration and a constant object declaration. These declarations can be made available to other compilation units through the context clause

with *winning*;

In this way a package or the main procedure can make use of information declared in other packages.

Because package *winning* is independent of package *student_io*, it does not need a context clause. The main procedure, on the ther hand, depends on both the packages *student_io* and *winning* and so both are given in its context clause. The two with clauses and the two use clauses can be amalgamated to give the context clause

with *student_io, winning*; **use** *student_io, winning*;

A with clause must precede its corresponding use clause. Because both the packages are listed in the use as well as the with clause, we can refer, in the main procedure, to *put, get, put_line, list* and *win_list* instead of having to refer to *student_io.put, student_io.get, student_io.put_line, winning.list* and *winning.win_list*.

We now see that an Ada program is composed of separate units, some of which may be existing library packages. In Program 12.1 the units are package *winning*, the library package *student_io* and procedure *look_up*, together with package *standard* which is automatically part of all Ada programs. The built-in types such as *integer* and *character* are declared in package *standard*.

Let us now look at the general form of a package specification:

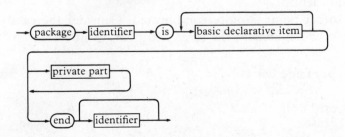

A basic declarative item can include an object declaration, a type declaration, a subprogram declaration, a subtype declaration, a package declaration or a use clause, but may not include the declaration of a subprogram or package body. A package or subprogram declaration is just a package or subprogram specification followed by a semi-colon.

The purpose and the form of the private part and the reason for the restriction on what may be declared in a package specification will all be given in the next chapter.

12.4   Use clauses

Before we go on to deal with package bodies it is necessary to say a few words of caution about the effect of use clauses.

First the good news. The introduction of a use clause has no effect on local declarations. If, for example, we have the declarations

```
package one is
    first, second : integer;
end one;

with one; use one;
procedure main is
    first : Boolean;
begin
    .
    .
    .
end main;
```

then, in the main procedure, the local declaration of the Boolean variable *first* takes precedence over the declaration in the package of the integer variable *first*. Hence, to refer in the main procedure to the integer variable we have to give it its full name of *one.first*, even though *one* has been mentioned in a use clause.

This is an important point. It means that we can introduce the contents of an external package into a package or subprogram without any fear that its introduction will interfere with any of our locally declared identifiers.

The other point is more complicated. Consider the case of two packages which contain the same identifier, as in

```
package one is
    first, second : integer;
end one;
```

```
package two is
  first, third : Boolean;

end two;
with one, two; use one, two;
procedure main is
begin
  .
  .
  .
end main;
```

The full names *one.first* and *two.first* must be used in the main procedure to determine which of the two possible identifiers is being referred to. The system will not determine from the context whether an integer or Boolean variable is needed. Hence we can refer to *second* and *third* in the main procedure, but it would be an error to try to refer to *first*.

The exception to this rule is when the two conflicting identifiers both refer to subprograms or to enumeration literals. In this case the context in which they are used will decide which of the possibilities is meant. This is the overloading feature which we met in chapter 6. Once again you are advised not to introduce new examples of over-loading into your programs until you are experienced in the use of Ada. Even then overloading should not be used lightly.

In large programs which make extensive use of packages, it is often preferable to give the full name for infrequently used types and objects made available through a context clause, rather than to use the abbreviated form. This is to make clear to the reader where the declaration took place. Where this is not done, it is good practice to give the information in a comment. The exception to this is when the identifiers are well known, such as those declared in *standard* and *student_io*.

Exercises

1. Assuming that the following package of astronomical data is available, write a program which asks questions such as

   How far is the Earth from the Sun?

   Your program should accept answers which are within 10 % of the correct value and otherwise request the user to try again.

   package *astronomical* **is**
     light_year : **constant** *real* := 5.88E12 --miles

```
parsec : constant real := 3.26 --light years
nearest_star : constant real := 4.31 --light years
earth_to_sun : constant real := 9.3E7 --miles
earth_to_moon : constant real := 2.391E5 --miles
end astronomical;
```

13

Package Bodies

13.1 Hiding information

Let us return to our lottery program. Information about the winning tickets was held in a package where it could be accessed from the rest of the program. In the example, function *in_list* was used to search the list of winning numbers. Because this function was used only to access information in the package, it should really have been declared within the package instead of in the main procedure.

Because we still want to call this function from the main procedure, its name must be visible from outside the package. This means that it should be in the visible part of the package, i.e. in the package specification. Subprogram bodies may not, however, be given in a package specification, but then to call a subprogram we do not need to know about its internal details. All we need to know is its name, the number and type of its parameters and, in the case of a function, the type of its returned value. This information is given in a subprogram declaration.

Hence the declaration of function *in_list* will go in the package specification, while the body of function *in_list* will go in the package body, where it will be hidden from the rest of the program.

A package specification must be given before its body and all identifiers declared in the specification are automatically available in the body. This leads to the following package:

package *winning* **is**
    type *list* **is array** (*positive* **range** < >) **of** *natural*;
    win_list : **constant** *list* := (2546, 3479, 4321, 5173,
                            9716, 9837);
    function *in_list*(*number* : *natural*;
                   search_list : *list*) **return** *Boolean*;
end *winning*;

package body *winning* **is**

```
             function in_list(number : natural;
                             search_list : list) return Boolean is
          begin
             --find if number is in the list
             for pos in search_list'range loop
                --note multiple exit from loop
                if number = search_list(pos) then
                   return true;
                end if;
             end loop;
             return false;
          end in_list;
       end winning;
```

Because it appears in the visible part, function *in_list* can be called from the main procedure in exactly the same way as before.

This is the first time we have used a subprogram declaration. It is possible, but not necessary, for all subprograms to be declared in two parts. The subprogram declaration gives all the information necessary to call the subprogram, while the body also gives the information about how the subprogram is implemented. The subprogram specifications used in the subprogram declaration and body must be equivalent, and every subprogram declaration must have a corresponding subprogram body.

A package body can include object, type, subtype, subprogram and package declarations, and use clauses, together with, unlike a package specification, the declarations of subprogram and package bodies. Its syntax is

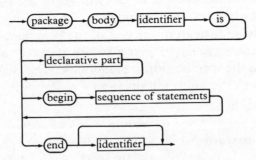

The optional sequence of statements is used to initialise the package. It is frequently not needed because most variables can be initialised when they are declared, but, to support the idea of information hiding, it is important that objects declared within a package are initialised in one of these two ways so that users of the package can correctly assume that the package is ready for use without taking any special action.

When we design a package the general idea is to put the minimum necessary information into the visible part of a package and to hide away as much information as possible in the package body. Using this principle, let us re-design package *winning* by considering the information the main lottery procedure needs to know. The list of winning numbers is accessed only by function *in_list* and so can be hidden in the package body. This improves security significantly, for it would seem desirable to keep information about the winning numbers hidden from unauthorised access.

The revised version of the program is

PROGRAM 13.1

```
package winning is
   function in_list(number : natural) return Boolean;
   --search a list in the body for number
end winning;

package body winning is
   type list is array (positive range < >) of natural;
   win_list : constant list := (2546, 3479, 4321, 5173,
                                9716, 9837);

   function in_list(number : natural) return Boolean is
   begin
      --find if number is in the non-local win_list
      for pos in win_list'range loop
         --note multiple exit from loop
         if number = win_list(pos) then
            return true;
         end if;
      end loop;
      return false;
   end in_list;
end winning;

with student_io, winning; use student_io;
procedure look_up is
   ticket_number : natural;
begin
   --read ticket number and check if it wins a prize
   put("What is your number?");
   get(ticket_number);
   if winning.in_list(ticket_number) then
```

```
          put_line("Well done, you have won a prize");
     else
          put_line("Sorry, better luck next time");
     end if;
end look_up;
```

A context clause makes available identifiers declared in a package specification but not identifiers declared in a package body. This means that only the function *in_list* is visible from outside package *winning* and so the only way in which the list of winning numbers can be accessed is through a call of this function. The list is completely protected from being accessed in any other way, and because the list is no longer a parameter of the function, a program using the package cannot even find out how many winning numbers there are.

13.2　Further examples

In Program 10.2 we used procedures *get_line* and *get_word* respectively to read a line of text and to get the next word from the line. The drawbacks of not being able to hide information about the line structure have already been discussed and so let us now try to design a suitable package.

We need a procedure to get the next line of text, a procedure to extract the next word from the line, ways of indicating both the end of the text and when there are no more words in a line, and a procedure to print the contents of the current line. No other information needs to be visible outside the package. Even the line itself can be hidden.

A possible package specification is

```
package lines is
     procedure next_line;
     --read the next line
     procedure get_word(the_word : out string);
     --get the next word from the current line
     function end_of_text return Boolean;
     --true when all lines have been read
     function more_words return Boolean;
     --true if there could be more words in the line
     procedure write_current_line;
end lines;
```

All the information about the line is hidden inside the package body and can be accessed only through calls of the subprograms declared in the package specification. The package body is given below. It uses subprograms declared in package *student_io*, but because these subprograms are not required in the package specification of *lines*, *student_io* is mentioned only in the context clause for the body of *lines*, not in the context clause for it specification. This and related points are discussed more fully in section 15.1.

```
with student_io; use student_io;
package body lines is
   line : string(1 .. 80);
   line_length : natural range 0 .. line'last := 0;
   char_no : natural range 0 .. line'last + 1 : 0;
   --char_no is the current position in line

   function letter(ch : character) return Boolean is
   begin
      --determine if the character is a letter
      return ch in 'a' .. 'z' or ch in 'A' .. 'Z';
   end letter;

   function lower_case(ch : character) return character is
   begin
      --convert upper case letters to lower case
      if ch in 'A' .. 'Z' then
         return character'val(characer'pos(ch) +
                  character'ois('a') - character'pos('A'));
      else
         return ch;
      end if;
   end lower_case;

   procedure next_line is
   begin
      --get the next line
      get_line(line, line_length);
      char_no := 0;
   end next_line;

   procedure get_word(the_word : out string) is
      pos : positive := the_word'first;
   begin
      --get next word from line starting at char_no + 1
      --the size of the_word depends on the actual parameter
      --find start of next word
      loop
         char_no := char_no + 1;
```

```
      exit when char_no = line_length or
              letter(line(char_no00;
   end loop;
   --scan the next word
   --ignore words which cannot fit into the_word
   the_word := (the_word'range => ' ');
   while char_no < = line_length and then
           letter(line(char_no)) loop
      if pos < = the_word'last then
        the_word(pos) := lower_case(line(char_no));
      elsif pos = the_word'last + 1 then
        --word too long, reset the_word
        the_word := (the_word'range => ' ');
      end if;
      char_no := char_no + 1; pos := pos + 1;
   end loop;
 end get_word;

 function end_of_text return Boolean is
 begin
   --check for terminating line
   return line_length = 1 and then line(1) = '.';
 end end_of_text;

 function more_words return Boolean is
 begin
   --can there be more words on the line?
   return char_no < line_length;
 end more_words;

 procedure write_current_line is
 begin
   put_line(line(1 .. line_length));
 end write_current_line;
end lines;
```

Variables *line, line_length* and *char_no* are accessed by the visible procedures and functions as non-local variables rather than as parameters so that they can remain hidden from outside the package. The need to be able to hide objects within a package body takes priority over the usual rule that procedures should not access and change non-local variables.

We should be even stricter with functions. They should not be allowed to change the value of a non-local variable. Because their parameters must be **in** mode, this means that a function call can then interact with the rest of a program only through its returned value. If we feel that it is necessary for a function to change a non-local variable then we should rewrite the function as a procedure.

Because they are used only within the package, the two functions *letter* and *lower_case* are declared in the package body but are not given in the package specification. This means that they cannot be called from outside the package. Package bodies can therefore contain useful subprograms whose existence is hidden from the rest of the program.

Let us now see how packages can be used in a re-worked version of Program 10.2. When we design a package it is important to ensure that all the objects, types and subprograms declared within it are logically connected. Package *lines* has therefore dealt only with the structure of, and the operations on, a line of text. Program 10.2 also contained a list of special words and a function to search the list. They have been put into a second package because they have no logical connection with the operations on a line of text. Package *special_word* is very similar to package *winning* declared earlier in this chapter. This again shows that when we produce solutions to problems we can often build on what we have already rather than start from scratch.

PROGRAM 13.2

```
package special_word is
   subtype word is string(1 .. 5);
   function in_list(new_word : word) return Boolean;
   --in_list searches a list for occurrences of new_word
end special_word;
package body special_word is
   type special_list is array (positive range < >) of word;
word_list : constant special_list := ("begin", "else ", "end   ",
                "for  ", "if   ", "loop ", "then ", "while");
   function in_list(new_word : word) return Boolean is
   begin
      --find if new_word is in the non-local word_list
      for pos in word_list'range loop
        --note multiple exit from loop
        if new_word = word_list(pos) then
           return true;
        end if;
      end loop;
      return false;
   end in_list;
```

```
end special_word;

with student_io, lines, special_word;
use student_io, lines;
procedure find_words is
    --line manipulation subprograms declared in package lines
    next_word : special_word.word;
    word_found : Boolean := false;
begin
    --program to find occurrences of certain words in a text
    loop
        --read the next line
        next_line;
        exit when end_of_text;
        --take each word and check it against the special list
        word_found := false;
        while more_words loop
            get_word(next_word);
            --find if the word is in the list
            if special_word.in_list(next_word) then
                put_line(next_word);
                word_found := true;
            end if;
        end loop;
        if word_found then
            put_line("found in");
            write_current_line;
        end if;
    end loop;
end find_words;
```

Although the complete program is no simpler than the original version we have managed to split it into three parts connected only by small strictly-defined interfaces (the package specifications). We know that the only interactions which can occur between the different parts are through items which have been declared in these specifications.

This allows a person, or indeed three different people, to write the three parts separately. Once the problems to be solved by the two packages have been formulated, their solution is independent of the rest of the program. To write the main procedure we need to have information only about the specifications of the two packages, not about their bodies.

In our next example a stack package is declared. We want to use a stack of characters in a program, but we wish to hide all the details of the stack inside a package. Only the *push, pop* and *reset_stack* procedures and the functions *stack_is_empty* and *stack_top* are to be visible. A possible package is

```
package stack is
   --standard stack handling subprograms
   procedure push(x : character);
   procedure pop(x : out character);
   function stack_is_empty return Boolean;
   function stack_top return character;
   procedure reset_stack;
end stack;

with student_io; use student_io;
package body stack is
   type list is array (1 .. 100) of character;
   type char_stack is
      record
         item : list;
         top : natural := 0;
      end record;
   st : char_stack;

   procedure push(x : character) is
   begin
      --add character to stack
      if st.top = 100 then
         put_line("Stack is already full");
      else
         st.top := st.top + 1;
         st.item(st.top) := x;
      end if;
   end push;

   procedure pop(x : out character) is
   begin
      --remove top character from stack
      if st.top = 0 then
         put_line("Stack is empty");
      else
         x := st.item(st.top);
         st.top := st.top - 1;
      end if;
   end pop;

   function stack_is_empty return Boolean is
```

```
        begin
          return st.top = 0;
        end stack_is_empty;

        function stack_top return character is
        begin
          --return top character of stack
          if st.top = 0 then
            put_line("Stack is empty");
            return ' ';
          else
            return st.item(st.top);
          end if;
        end stack_top;

        procedure reset_stack is
        begin
          --reset stack to be empty
          st.top := 0;
        end reset_stack;
      end stack;
```

The subprograms *push*, *pop*, etc. can be made visible to other units by a context clause and characters can then be added or removed from the stack by statements such as

push('a'); *push*('b'); *pop*(*val1*); *pop*(*val2*);

If *val1* and *val2* are character variables this statement sequence will give them the values 'b' and 'a' respectively.

The actual stack, called *st*, is hidden inside the package body. Exactly how it has been implemented is therefore not known to units which use the package.

13.3 Changing package bodies

In program 13.2 information on how to call function *in_list* is available to the main procedure, but information on how it works is hidden. In fact it uses a very simple search method called linear search, in which we start at one end of a list and scan components until we either find the item or come to the end of the list. The disadvantage of this method is that if we double the length of a list then the search will take twice as long. A more efficient method is therefore required when long lists are being searched.

A package can interact with the rest of a program only through its visible part. Any changes to a package body can therefore affect the rest of the program only by changing items in the visible part of the package. In package *special_word* the interaction with outside is that function *in_list* is passed a value of type *word* and returns a *Boolean* result.

The body of function *in_list* is hidden inside the package body. If we change the body of function *in_list* in such a way that it gives the same *Boolean* answer as before for each possible value of the *word* parameter, we can guarantee that this change will have no effect on the rest of the program. A person who has access only to the main procedure will not even be aware that a change has taken place.

This is exactly what we want if we are to design and implement large systems. It means that we can make changes to part of a large program, namely a package body, and know that the only effect that these changes can have on the rest of the program is through items declared in the package specification. We have a guarantee that there will be no other unforeseen side-effects. If package specifications are kept small, the interaction between packages is kept to a minimum. This then gives us a method of controlling how the different parts of large complex systems interact with one another.

As an example of this, let us change the method used in *in_list* from linear to the much faster binary search. Binary search has the restriction that it can only be used to search lists which are in order, but that is not a restriction here because the words in *word_list* are in alphabetical order.

Binary search works by first comparing the item which is being searched for with the component in the middle of the list. There are then three possibilities. You may be lucky and have a direct hit; otherwise you will find either that the value of the item is less than that of the middle component, in which case the item is in the first half of the list, or the value of the item is greater than the middle component, in which case the item is in the second half of the list.

After one comparison we have either found the required item or have halved the size of the list which needs to be considered. We proceed by taking the relevant half and looking at its middle component. In this way the list is again halved. This is continued until we either find what we are looking for or there are no components left to be considered.

Because each comparison halves the size of the list under consideration, we can quickly deal with all the possibilities. A list of 1000 components only needs a maximum of ten comparisons. Such a list would have required an average of 500 comparisons using our linear search function. With 1000 components in a list, our binary search function is therefore 50 times faster!

A binary search version of *in_list* is now given:

```
function in_list(new_word : word) return Boolean is
    middle : positive;
    low : positive := word_list'first;
    high : natural := word_list'last;
begin
    loop
        --find if new_word is in word_list(low .. high)
        middle := (low + high) / 2;
        if new_word < word_list(middle) then
            high := middle - 1;
            --range of new list is (low .. middle - 1)
        elsif new_word > word_list(middle) then
            low := middle + 1;
            --range of new list is (middle + 1 .. high)
        else
            --item found
            return true;
        end if;
        --range of new list is (low .. high)
        exit when low > high; --when list is empty
    end loop;
    return false;
end in_list;
```

Because the new version of *in_list* gives the same answers as before, replacing the old version by the new will not affect the rest of the program. With a list of eight components binary search is not necessary, but we are now ready to deal efficiently with a much longer list of special words.

13.4 Abstract data types

We have seen how packages can be used to bring together object, type and subprogram declarations and hide internal details. They can do more than that, however.

We have been using types such as *integer*, *character* and *real*, and have considered a type to be a range of values together with a set of operations which can take place on these values. Hence with the type *integer* we have the whole numbers and operations such as addition, subtraction, testing for equality, etc. We do not have to bother in our programs about how integers are represented in a computer or how operations such as multiplication take place. Such detail would not help us to use integers, but would only complicate matters.

With packages we can declare together types and subprograms. This gives us the ability to create new data types complete with their built-in operations. The exact way in which the type is represented and how the operations are to be carried out will be hidden in the package body. Users of the new type will only need to know how to declare objects and what operations are available. This will allow them to think about the type at an abstract level, just as a user of integers only needs to have an abstract idea of what an integer is.

Once such a new "abstract type" has been declared, it will be possible to use it in the solutions to problems in the same way as we can use any built-in type, but as the new types will be at a relatively high level and oriented towards particular problems, this should lead to more easily understood programs. Once we have declared objects of a new abstract type, we should never try to find out about their internal representation. Operations on the new objects should be carried out by the subprograms declared in the package defining the new type together with the operation of assignment and tests for equality and inequality which are automatically available. In that way the type is used in exactly the same way as any predefined type.

As an example of this new idea, let us again consider a stack. In the previous section we had a package which could be used to manipulate a single stack. We now want to be able to declare and manipulate several objects of type *stack*, just as we can declare and manipulate several objects of type *integer*. We want to think of a stack of items as an abstract concept which is to be implemented in some way. Once we have a stack data type, we will be able to declare objects of type *stack* and use operations such as *push* and *pop*.

In the following package specification a stack of characters is declared:

```
package char_stack is
   type values is array (1 .. 100) of character;
   type stack is
      record
         item : values;
         top : natural := 0;
      end record;
   procedure push(x : character; st : in out stack);
   procedure pop(x : out character; st : in out stack);
end char_stack;
```

We now have a stack type which can contain up to 100 characters. Two operations, *push* and *pop*, are available to manipulate objects of this type, but how *push* and *pop* are implemented is hidden from view in the package body.

Once the visible part of the package and the body have been declared, the type *stack* can be made available to other units by means of a context clause. We can then have declarations such as

> *op_stack, temporary : stack;*
> *op : character;*

and statements such as

> *push('+', op_stack); push('*', op_stack);*
> *push('a', temporary);*
> *pop(op, op_stack);*

After execution of these statements the *op_stack* and *temporary* stacks will each contain one item, while the value held in the character variable *op* will be an asterisk. If the package has been properly defined and objects are manipulated only through the built-in operations, then our use of the type will always be at a fairly high, abstract level.

A possible package body to fit the package specification is

```
with student_io; use student_io;
package body char_stack is
   procedure push(x : character; st : in out stack) is
   begin
      --add character to stack
      if st.top = 100 then
         put_line("Stack is already full");
      else
         st.top := st.top + 1;
         st.item(st.top) := x;
      end if;
   end push;

   procedure pop(x : out character; st : in out stack) is
   begin
      --remove top character from the stack
      if st.top = 0 then
         put_line("Stack is empty");
      else
         x := st.item(st.top);
         st.top := st.top - 1;
```

  end if;
  end *pop;*
 end *char_stack;*

Alternative package bodies are possible of course.

 A problem remains. Although we can urge the user to change a stack only by the operations of *push* and *pop*, this advice may be ignored. It is, for example, still possible to add an element to a stack by statements such as

  op_stack.top := *op_stack.top* + 1;
  op_stack.item(*op_stack.top*) := ' + ';

instead of using

  push(' + ', *op_stack*);

 Although this should not be done it has not been made impossible. If we change the internal components of a stack in this way there is no guarantee that we are doing so in a way consistent with the defined stack operations and, as we are at a more detailed level, it is much easier to make mistakes. Most importantly, we are no longer considering a stack to be a new abstract type with its own operations, but are becoming involved with the details of its implementation.

 If the designer of a package feels that access to internal details should be restricted, it should be possible to design a package in such a way that this rule can be enforced.

 Ada allows us to declare types to be private. The names of private types can be used outside the package, but their internal structure can be accessed only from within the package body. The specification of type *stack* now becomes

  package *char_stack* **is**
   type *stack* **is private;**
   procedure *push*(*x* : *character*; *st* : **in out** *stack*);
   procedure *pop*(*x* : **out** *character*; *st* : **in out** *stack*);
   private
    type *values* **is array** (1 .. 100) **of** *character*;
    type *stack* **is**
     record
      item : *values*;
      top : *natural* := 0;
     end record;
  end *char_stack;*

The package body can be declared exactly as before.

Because the identifier *stack* is to be visible outside the package and because it is used in the procedure specifications, it must be declared in the visible part of the package. Because however, it is declared to be private, no details of its structure are given there. The full declaration is given in the private part of the package specification. The general form of a private part is

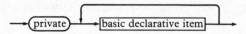

Identifiers introduced in the private part of a stack specification are, like identifiers declared in the package body, not visible outside the package. Details of the structure of the type *stack* cannot therefore be used outside the package. We can still declare stack objects such as

op_stack, *temporary* : *stack*;

but the only operations now available on these stacks are *push* and *pop*. It is no longer possible to access the stack contents in any other way. The type *values* is required in the definition of the stack and, as it does not have to be seen from outside, it is declared in the private rather than in the visible part of the package specification.

We have now achieved our aim of creating a new data type which has the properties of a predefined data type. We can declare objects of this type and can perform operations on these objects. We are, however, unable to make use of any knowledge which we may have concerning their internal structure.

13.5 Summary

Understanding a program is much easier when the declarations of logically related objects, types and subprograms are kept together instead of being scattered throughout a program. Because packages enable this to be done, they form the basis for the logical organisation of Ada programs.

The main problem with large programs is their size and complexity. We therefore want to be able to divide them into self-contained units which can interact with one another only through small, strictly defined interfaces.

The Ada package allows us to do this. A large Ada program is written as a series of compilation units, each of which usually contains a main procedure, a package declaration or a package body. Each package has a relatively small specification, which is its interface with the other units. The implementation of the package is then hidden from view in the package body. How the different compilation units depend on one another is specified by their context clauses. In this way any interaction between units is kept to a minimum and can clearly be seen.

The idea of collecting together related declarations can be extended to the idea of abstract data types where a new type and its associated operations are defined in a package. The internal structure of the new type is hidden from view and so objects of the new type can be manipulated only as a whole using the defined operations. Because the new types can be at a fairly high level and be oriented towards the problem being solved, this allows us to think about solutions to problems at a conceptual level rather than always being forced to think about implementation details.

Exercises

1. Why, when we design a package, do we put the minimum amount of information into the package specification and hide as much information as possible in the package body?

2. Extend the stack abstract data type described in section 13.4 so that the operations *stack_is_empty*, *stack_top* and *reset_stack* are also available.

3. If instead of a stack of characters we needed a stack of integers, how easy would it be to modify our stack package so that it dealt with integers rather than characters?

4. In chapter 11 exercise 3 we constructed a type declaration for rational numbers. Outline the design of a package to implement the abstract data type of rational numbers. The operations of addition, subtraction, multiplication and division should be made available for objects of type *rational_number*.

   Should *rational_number* be a private type?

5. In program 13.2 we read several lines of text and searched for occurrences of certain words. If the problem was extended so that we had to search for occurrences of any of the reserved words in Ada (they are given in appendix 1), what changes, if any, would have to be made to each of the following:

   (a) the package specification and body of *special_word*,
   (b) the package specification and body of *lines*,
   (c) the main program.

6. In a stack items are added or removed from the top of the stack. In a queue items are added to the end of the queue and are removed from the front. Outline the definition of a queue abstract data type.

14

Visibility and existence

14.1 Visibility

The visibility of identifiers has been discussed informally in earlier chapters; some more details are now given here. Ada's visibility rules are quite complicated but as long as we do not try to be too clever many details can be ignored until we wish to claim expert status.

The most important rules are that all identifiers must be declared before they can be used, and that an identifier can only be used where it is visible. When identifiers are declared in the declarative part of a subprogram or package they are visible from the end of their declaration to the end of that subprogram or package. They are also visible within any inner subprogram or package. Hence in the following example identifiers declared within procedure *outer* are also visible within procedure *enclosed*, but identifiers declared in procedure *enclosed* cannot be seen from outside that procedure.

```
procedure outer is
    val : constant positive := 1;
    ch : character;
    procedure enclosed(flag : Boolean) is
        one : positive := val;
        val : constant Boolean := true;
        answer : Boolean := val;
        ein : positive := outer.val;
    begin
        .
        .
        .
    end enclosed;
```

begin

.

.

.

end *outer*;

We say that identifiers are local to the subprogram or package in which they are declared and are global or non-local to any inner subprogram or package. Hence *val, ch* and *enclosed* are local to procedure *outer* and non-local to procedure *enclosed*, while *flag, one, answer, ein* and the Boolean constant *val* are local to procedure *enclosed*. We can always refer to both local and non-local identifiers, but it is good practice to declare identifiers to be as local as possible so that subprograms and packages can be self-contained.

The identifier *val* has been declared as a positive constant within procedure *outer* and as a Boolean constant within procedure *enclosed*. Because an identifier becomes visible only after it has been declared, the first declaration in procedure *enclosed*

> *one* : *positive* := *val*;

although it is not good practice, is legal and gives *one* an initial value of 1. Once the Boolean constant has been declared however, there is a conflict as to which declaration any use of the identifier *val* belongs. The more local declaration takes precedence and so the positive constant identifier *val* is hidden by the Boolean constant identifier *val*. If we still wish to use the positive constant in *enclosed* it has to be referred to by its full name of *outer.val*.

Two instances of the same identifier may not be declared in the same declarative part unless they are both subprograms with different parameters or are enumeration literals. This is the overloading feature and once again it is recommended that you do not introduce overloaded identifiers into your programs until you are experienced, and even then only when there is a very good reason. Straightforward programs are easier to read and understand and are much more likely to be correct than complicated ones.

Finally, an identifier cannot be used within its own declaration. This prohibits seemingly sensible declarations such as

> *border* : *string*(1 .. 40) := (*border'range* => '***'); --illegal

The visibility rules of packages differ from subprograms in that identifiers declared in the visible part of the package specification can be made visible outside the package. Context clauses and the effect on visibility of the use clause have already been fully discussed. The declarative parts of a package specification and its body should be considered together as one single declarative part. This means that all identifiers declared in the package specification are visible in the package body.

14.2 The life-time of objects

Objects are represented in Ada programs by identifiers and the visibilty of an identifier can always be determined by looking at the text of a program. Because this property does not depend on the execution of the program we say that it is static.

As well as wanting to know in which region of a program text an object can be used, we wish to know when, during the execution of a program, an object exists. During execution objects are created, i.e., are allocated storage space. They may then be given values. Later the storage space may be "de-allocated", in which case the object ceases to exist. The life-time of an object is concerned with its existence during the execution of a program. It is a dynamic property.

An Ada program consists of a series of compilation units. One compilation unit contains the main procedure and we shall suppose the others to contain packages. Using the following program skeleton as a guide, let us consider when storage is allocated to objects and when objects are given values.

```
package outer is
  visible : natural := 0;
  procedure examine(answer : out Boolean);
end outer;

package body outer is
  invisible : positive;

  procedure examine(answer : out Boolean) is
    inner : character;
    loc : integer;
  begin
    .
    .
    .
  end examine;

begin
  invisible := 1;
end outer;
```

```
with outer;
procedure main is
   result : Boolean;
begin
   .
   .
   .
   outer.examine(result);
   .
   .
   .
end main;
```

Here we have three compilation units: the declaration of package *outer*, the body of package *outer* and procedure *main*.

A program consists of instructions which are to be executed and objects which are to be manipulated by these instructions. Before a program can be executed the instructions in all the compilation units making up the program must be loaded into the main store of the computer. Execution of the program may then start, but before the main procedure can be executed all the packages on which it depends must be initialised. In this example this involves the declaration and the body of package *outer*. Storage is allocated to the objects declared in the declarative part of package *outer* and these objects are assigned any initial values. This act of reserving space for the objects and giving them their initial values is called "elaborating" the declarations. If a declarative part contains several declarations then they are elaborated in the order in which they are given in the declarative part.

Elaboration of the declarative part of the package declaration of *outer* results in storage being allocated to the variable object *visible* and it being initialised to the value 0. Elaboration of the package body consists of first elaborating its declarative part and then executing its sequence of statements. Elaboration of the declarative part of the body results in storage being allocated to the object *invisible* and its value being left undefined. Execution of the sequence of statements in the body then results in *invisible* being given the value 1.

We then start execution of the main procedure. This involves elaborating its declarative part first, so space is reserved for the Boolean variable *result*. Because it does not have an initial value, its value is left undefined. Execution then continues with the first statement in the main procedure.

During execution of procedure *main* we come across a call of procedure *examine* and so this procedure is entered. It is only when procedure *examine* is entered that its declarative part is elaborated and space is allocated to the objects *answer*, *inner* and *loc*. When we eventually return from executing procedure *examine*, this space is de-allocated. Objects local to a subprogram come into existence only when the subprogram is entered and are destroyed when we return from the subprogram. Objects declared in the declarative part of a package like *outer* on the other hand remain in existence throughout the execution of the program.

When a subprogram is called recursively new "incarnations" of the local objects are created each time the subprogram is called. Let us look at this through a call of the *factorial* function described in section 7.8.

```
function factorial(n : natural) return positive is
begin
    --calculate n factorial
    if n > 1 then
        return n * factorial(n − 1);
    else
        return 1;
    end if;
end factorial;
```

The effect of the call

$$y := factorial(3);$$

is to enter function *factorial* and to allocate space for the **in** parameter *n*, which is given the value 3. During execution of *factorial* the function is called again, this time with actual parameter 2. The effect of this call is to enter the function and to again allocate space for the **in** parameter *n*, which this time is given the value 2.

During this execution of *factorial* the function is again called and space is allocated for a third incarnation of *n*, which is given the value 1. Three objects called *n*, each with different values, are therefore simultaneously in existence. When we return from the different calls of *factorial*, space is de-allocated in the reverse order in which it was originally allocated.

This is just the order in which objects are pushed onto and popped from a stack; the last item added is the first to be removed. It should therefore come as no surprise to learn that the allocation of space to local objects in a subprogram is done using a stack. This is usually referred to as "stack storage allocation".

Exercises

1. Distinguish between the visibility and the life-time of an object.

2. We say that variables exist at run-time when they have storage space allocated. What important difference is there between the life-time of a variable declared in the declarative part of a package and one declared in the declarative part of a subprogram?

15

Program structure

15.1 Library units

It is now time to look in detail at the structure of an Ada program. We know that a program consists of a series of compilation units, and that the interdependence of these units is specified by their context clauses. Let us consider the following program skeleton:

```
with useful_things; use useful_things;
package outer is
    .
    .
    .
end outer;

with student_io; use student_io;
package body outer is
    .
    .
    .
end outer;

with student_io, outer; use student_io, outer;
procedure start is
    .
    .
    .
end start;
```

This program consists of the library packages *student_io* and *useful_things*, the package *outer* and a main procedure, together, of course, with the package *standard*, which is automatically part of all Ada programs.

A compilation unit is a context clause followed either by a library unit or by a secondary unit. A library unit can be a procedure body or a package declaration, and a secondary unit can be a package body. A package body is called a secondary unit as each body must be associated with a corresponding package declaration.

In our example outline program we have at least five library units, the packages *student_io*, *useful_things*, *outer* and *standard* and the procedure *start*. We have as secondary units the package bodies of *outer*, *student_io* and *standard*, and we may also have a package body for *useful_things*, but that information is hidden from us. The library packages *student_io* and *useful_things* may depend on other library units, but that information is also hidden.

Packages *student_io* and *useful_things* are what we have called library packages and are assumed to exist somewhere, as yet unspecified, in the system. It is interesting to note that, according to the definition of a compilation unit, it is not only library packages which are defined to be library units; so too are packages such as *outer*. As far as Ada is concerned, there is no difference between an existing library package and a package such as *outer* which is presented to the compiler along with the main procedure.

All the units in an Ada program make up what is known as a program library. Units such as library packages are assumed to be already in the library while other units such as, in this case, the package declaration and body of *outer* and procedure *start*, are added to the library when they are compiled.

The structure of the program and how the different units fit together is indicated by the following diagram:

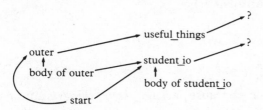

Let us consider what happens when execution of the program is initiated. Before execution of the main procedure can begin, the packages on which it depends, *standard*, *student_io* and *outer*, must be elaborated. Before the specification of package *outer* can be elaborated, the specification of package *useful_things* has to be elaborated. Before the body of package *outer* can be elaborated, the specifications of *outer* and package *student_io* have to be elaborated. A package specification must always be elaborated before the corresponding package body. Before packages *student_io* and *useful_things* are elaborated, the specifications of any packages on which they depend will have to be elaborated, but we do not have details of this because their context clauses, although they exist, are hidden from view. After all, for us to use a package there is no need to know about the packages on which it might depend.

We can now see that even in a relatively small program a considerable chain of package elaborations takes place before execution of the main procedure can be initiated.

Because *student_io* is required by procedure *start* and by the package body of *outer*, it must be elaborated before either of these units. Despite being mentioned in more than one context clause, it is only elaborated once.

Although procedure *start* depends on package *outer*, which in turn depends on package *useful_things* we do not have to mention *useful_things* in the context clause of procedure *start*. Only packages which are used directly need be mentioned in a context clause. Thus we can assume from their context clauses that both the main procedure and the package body of *outer* directly depend on package *student_io*.

A context clause given with a package specification does not have to be repeated with the package body because everything available to a package specification is automatically available to its body. It would not have been an error to have written a fuller context clause for the package body of *outer*:

> **with** *student_io*, *useful_things*; **use** *student_io*, *useful_things*;
> **package body** *outer* **is**
> .
> .
> .
> **end** *outer*;

but it was not necessary because package *useful_things* is automatically available to the body, having been given in the context clause of the package specification. In this example the body of *outer* depends on package *student_io*, but the specification of *outer* does not. Hence *student_io* is given in the context clause of the body and not in the context clause of the package specification.

15.2 Separate compilation

When we develop large programs, or even relatively small ones, we do not do so all in one step. To make the project manageable we need to be able to split the problem into self-contained parts. We have seen how packages can be used to divide large programs logically into more manageable units. Compilation units are the means by which we can divide large programs physically into manageable units.

The package therefore plays the central role in both the physical and the logical separation of large programs into a series of smaller, self-contained units which can be developed separately before being put together to form a complete program.

As the name implies, each compilation unit can be compiled separately. This is not the same as compiling it independently, for each compilation unit depends on the library units mentioned in its context clause. These library units must already have been compiled and be present in the program library before compilation of the new unit takes place. If the compilation is successful, the new unit will be added to the program library.

The program text presented to the compiler can consist of one or more compilation units. The effect of presenting several compilation units together is the same as presenting each one separately, but in the same order. The order is important because a compilation unit can be compiled only after all the library units on which it depends have been compiled.

Separate compilation makes it possible to test a new package, together with the units mentioned in its context clause, separately from the rest of a program. To do this we write a small main program to "drive" the package. This program might, for example, call the subprograms in the package with suitably chosen values for the parameters and then check that the returned values are correct. Once we are sure that a package is working correctly it can be mentioned in the context clause of other packages so that they can be tested in turn. Part of this test will be to ensure that the interface between the packages works correctly. In this way large tested programs can be systematically built up and we are never faced with the problem of a huge monolithic untested program.

Another common situation where the ability to compile packages separately gives significant advantages is when we have compiled and linked together all the units making up a complete program and are now testing the final program with sample data. During the tests we find an error which we manage to trace to a mistake in one of the compilation units. We correct the mistake and wish to continue the test runs. The whole program does not have to be recompiled and retested, only those parts which depend on the modified unit.

Let us consider the outline program from the previous section. The diagram showing the interdependence of the different units is again given for reference.

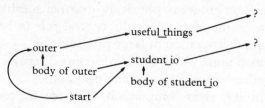

If the error was in the specification of package *outer* then only the specification and body of package *outer* and procedure *start* would have to be recompiled. As packages *student_io* and *useful_things* do not depend on *outer* there is no need to recompile them.

If the error had been in the specification of *useful_things* then, after the error had been corrected, the specification and body (if any) of *useful_things* would have had to be recompiled followed by the specification and body of package *outer*, which would in turn require the main procedure to be recompiled.

It might seem from this that any change is going to require most of a program to be recompiled. In large programs however, the library units are likely to be clustered in logically related groups and any modifications will require only other members of the group to be recompiled.

The main advantage of separate compilation is realised when the program modification has to be made to the body of a package rather than to its specification. A package body can be compiled separately from its specification, although the specification has to be compiled before the body. Compilation units which depend on a package can only see, and can therefore only depend on, the specification of a package, not on the body.

If in our example the error was found in the body of package *outer*, and this body was then modified in such a way that no change to the package specification was required, only the body of package *outer* would have to be recompiled. All the other compilation units could remain as they were.

This means that the body of a package can be completely changed and then recompiled and, as long as the changes do not affect the package specification and hence how the package is seen and used from outside, the package specification and the other units which depend on the package do not need to be changed in any way. The other units will not even be aware that the body has been modified.

When we are dealing with large programs consisting of many compilation units, this ability to change and then recompile some units without having to recompile the whole program can be very important and save a lot of time.

When compilation units are successfully recompiled they replace the earlier version in the program library. It would be quite easy for a programmer to forget to recompile one of the units affected by a change in some other unit. This must not be allowed to happen.

Associated with the program library is a library file, which contains information about the library and secondary units. One important piece of information is the date and time at which each unit was last compiled. This is then used to check that no compiled unit is used after another library unit on which it depends has been recompiled.

The creation, compilation and execution of Ada programs does not occur in a vacuum, but in a helpful environment of useful routines which will automatically perform checks such as this. This helpful environment is called the Ada Programming Support Environment or APSE for short.

It is the APSE which enables us to create and maintain program libraries, determine their contents and allow units from one library to be re-used in the creation of another library.

15.3 Using existing components

If we are asked to write a program to solve a particular problem we can either start writing the program from scratch or, after decomposing the initial problem into a series of subproblems, look to see if any of these subproblems have already been solved.

The abstract data types required might, for example, have already been implemented as part of the solution to some earlier problem and other useful subprograms or packages might have been written by other people.

Most computer installations will have collections of useful Ada subprograms and packages, and it is straightforward to incorporate such packages as library units in any new program library we are creating.

New programs, especially new large programs, are not usually created from scratch but have substantial parts built from existing components. This has given rise to hopes that it will be possible for programs to be manufactured from reliable and tested software components bought "off the shelf" from your local software store.

The Ada package is well suited to serving as a software component.

The specification of the package indicates the effect of the package. Its text can be shown to potential customers. Exactly how the package is implemented, i.e. the package body, will not be shown, although some of the algorithms used in implementing the package might be described.

15.4 Reverse Polish example

Let us now develop a program in which we assume that a library package called *stack*, such as the one described in section 13.2, already exists in our program library.

In chapter 6 we produced a simple calculator program. Evaluation took place from left to right, with no brackets being allowed and the normal precedence of the operators being ignored. Normally when we write arithmetic expressions we use what are called infix operators, i.e. operators which occur between two operands, as in

$a + b / c$

Infix operators require the use of brackets and an order of precedence of the operators to indicate the required order of evaluation. As an alternative we could use postfix operators where the operator comes after the operands on which it operates:

$a + b$ becomes $a\ b\ +$
b / c becomes $b\ c\ /$
$a + b / c$ becomes $a\ b\ c\ /\ +$
$(a + b) / c$ becomes $a\ b\ +\ c\ /$

Expressions written using postfix operators are said to be in "reverse Polish notation". Such expressions are not very convenient for human beings to use, which is why they are not in everyday use, but they have the advantage that they can be evaluated with no need for either brackets or a precedence for the operators.

To evaluate a reverse Polish expression we use a stack. The expression is scanned from the left and each time an operand is encountered its value is pushed onto the stack. When a binary operator is encountered the top two values on the stack are taken and are replaced by the result obtained by applying the operator to them. (Although unary operators can be dealt with we shall not consider them here.)

Once the whole expression has been scanned in this way we are left with a single value on the stack. This is the result of evaluating the expression.

The infix expression

$7 - (5 + 1) / 2$

is written in reverse Polish as

7 5 1 + 2 / −

and evaluation occurs as follows:

7	
7 5	
7 5 1	+
7 6	
7 6 2	/
7 3	−
4	
Stack contents	operator

When the operator + is encountered the top two values are 5 and 1, so they are replaced by the value 6. When the operator / is encountered the top two values are 6 and 2, so they are replaced by the result 3. Finally the − operator acts on 7 and 3 to give the answer 4.

If we wish to produce a calculator program which can deal with the precedence of operators and with brackets the easiest way is first to convert the infix expression to reverse Polish and then evaluate the reverse Polish expression as just described.

Let us now consider how the conversion can be done. To keep the problem relatively simple we shall assume that the operands are all single letters and that the infix expression is correctly formed. Our task is to write a program to convert a series of characters such as

$a - (b + c) / d$

into the equivalent reverse Polish form

$a\ b\ c + d\ / -$

The first thing to note about the reverse Polish form is that the order of the operands is unchanged from the infix expression. The order of the operators, on the other hand, has been changed so that they are now in the order in which they are to be used. The operands are not going to cause any problem, while the precedence of the operators is going to determine the order in which they are to appear in the reverse Polish expression.

There are several solutions to this problem and we shall consider one which involves a stack.

The input is read character by character. When an operand is scanned it is immediately output, while the output of an operator is delayed by keeping it on a stack. Exactly what happens when each character is input is described by the following outline algorithm:

```
          if the character is an operand then
              output the operand
          else if the character is an operator then
              loop until the stack is empty or a new operator has higher
                          precedence than the top operator on the stack
                  pop top operator from the stack and output it
              end loop
              push new operator onto the stack
          else
              skip character
          end if
```

Up till now we have ignored the question of brackets. An open bracket is pushed onto the stack and is then regarded as an operator with lower precedence than any other. This means that it cannot be popped from the stack by any of the other operators. A bracketed expression is therefore fully dealt with before any earlier operators which are still on the stack can be popped.

When a close bracket is encountered all operators up to the open bracket are popped from the stack and output. The open bracket is then removed from the stack. When we come to the end of the input all remaining operators are popped from the stack and output.

We are now in a position to write an outline algorithm for the whole conversion process:

```
          loop while there are still characters to be read
              get next character
              if the character is an operand then
                  output the operand
              else if the charcter is an operator then
                  loop until the stack is empty or the new operator has
                      higher precedence than the top operator on the stack
                      pop the top operator from the stack and output it
                  end loop
                  push new operator onto the stack
              else if the character is an open bracket then
                  push the open bracket onto the stack
              else if the character is a close bracket then
                  loop
                      pop the top operator from the stack
                      leave the loop if it was an open bracket
                      output the operator
                  end loop
```

```
      else
         skip character
      end if
   end loop
   loop while the stack is not empty
      pop operator and write it out
   end loop
```

To check that the outline algorithm works we must now trace it with suitably chosen data which will test each of the possible conditional paths. Among the cases to be considered are

Consecutive operators of equal precedence
Lower precedence operator followed by higher and vice versa
Bracketed expressions including nested brackets
Brackets at the beginning and at the end of expressions
Expressions containing no operators

These cases are tested by the following example expressions:

$$a + b - c \qquad a + b * c + d \quad a + (b + c) * d$$
$$(A + (B + C)) \,/\, D \qquad a \qquad\qquad ((a))$$

You should trace how each of these expressions is processed to improve your understanding of the action of the algorithm.

Once we are sure that our algorithm is working we can start implementing it in Ada. The algorithm has made extensive use of a stack of characters. Because we constructed a package to implement such a stack in chapter 13, all we need to do is add this package to our program library and make it available through a context clause. If it has already been compiled for use as part of some other program, we do not even have to recompile the package.

Because we have to compare the precedence of the different operators, we need to have some means of easily finding the precedence of each character operator, If we restrict the problem to dealing only with the multiplying and adding operators, the operators fall into the following groups:

the multiplying operators * and / (highest priority)
the adding operators + and − (next priority)
open bracket (lowest priority)

We can convert a character representing an operator into its appropriate priority value by table look-up using a constant array which has a character index and whose components give the relative priority. Looking at the table of ASCII characters in appendix 3, we see that the operator characters we are interested in are in the range '(' to '/', although this range does contain three characters we are not interested in. The look-up table can be put in the visible part of a package.

```
package convert is
  subtype op_char is character range '(' .. '/';
  --characters in this range are ( ) * + , − . /
  precedence : constant array (op_char) of natural :=
                  ('(' => 1,
                   '+' | '−' => 2,
                   '*' | '/' => 3,
                   ')' | ',' | '.' => 0);
end convert;
```

We are now in a position to write the main procedure. It closely follows the outline algorithm except that it is preferable to implement the complex if statement as a case statement. The implementation details of the stack and the determination of the precedence of the operators are hidden in packages, where they can be compiled separately and, as far as our final main program is concerned, can be regarded as high-level features of an extended Ada language.

PROGRAM 15.1

```
with student_io; use student_io;
with stack, convert; use stack, convert;
procedure rev_Polish is
  next_char : character;
  operator : op_char;
  --stack operations declared in package stack
  --precedence and op_char declared in convert
begin
  --read infix expression and convert it to reverse Polish
  while not end_of_line loop
    get(next_char);
    --deal with the different kinds of character
    case next_char is
      when 'a' .. 'z' | 'A' .. 'Z' =>
        put(next_char);
      when '+' | '−' | '*' | '/' =>
        loop
          exit when stack_is_empty or else
              precedence(next_char) > precedence(stack_top);
          pop(operator); put(operator);
        end loop;
        push(next_char);
      when '(' =>
```

```
        push('(');
    when ')' = >
        --pop operators up to and including'('
        loop
            pop(operator);
            exit when operator = '(';
            put(operator);
        end loop;
    when others = >
        null;
    end case;
end loop;
--output the remaining contents of the stack
while not stack_is_empty loop
    pop(operator); put(operator);
end loop;
new_line;
end rev_Polish;
```

Note that without looking at the package *convert* we cannot tell if the conversion from characters to priorities is performed by a function or by looking up a table. We could even change the method without having to change the text of the main procedure, although it would have to be recompiled.

This example shows us how previously written packages can be utilised in the production of new programs. It also shows how hiding the implementation of data structures such as the stack and the conversion routine allows us to remain at a higher, more abstract and problem-oriented level. In fact, the final implementation of the main procedure is not too different from our outline algorithm.

Exercises

1. If a package body is modified and then recompiled, do the packages and subprograms which depend on that package also have to be recompiled?

2. How many library units and how many secondary units are in Program 13.2? Outline the order in which the declarative parts of the library and secondary units are elaborated.

3. Outline the order in which the declarative parts of the library and secondary units in Program 15.1 are elaborated.

4. Extend Program 15.1 so that the relational operators >, < and = can be dealt with. Use the information in appendix 3 to obtain a suitable new definition for *op_char*.

16

Exceptions

16.1 Introduction

During the execution of a program an unusual or exceptional circumstance may arise. This may be due to some logical error in our algorithm, to unacceptable data being presented to the program, or just some situation which, although it may occur during normal execution, will occur only infrequently. If the ordinary program text was modified so that it could pick up and deal with all exceptional situations this could so complicate the text that the main flow of control would be hidden. This goes against our aim of writing programs which are easy to read and understand.

So that this does not happen, in Ada the handling of exceptional situations is separated from the normal flow of control. When an exceptional circumstance arises we say that "an exception is raised". Dealing with it is called "handling the exception". Exceptions can be raised in one of two ways, either automatically by the system when some error is detected, or by the programmer by means of an explicit raise statement such as

raise *constraint_error*;

Similarly we can either let the system deal with the exception or write a special "exception handler" to deal with it ourselves. When we let the system handle an exception the usual result is for the program to be terminated.

Some of the exceptions which can be raised automatically by the system have been described in earlier chapters. A fuller description is now given before we go on to describe how we can raise and deal with exceptions ourselves.

16.2 Predefined exceptions

The exceptions *constraint_error*, *numeric_error*, *program_error* and *storage_error* are part of the Ada language.

Several examples of how a *constraint_error* exception can be raised have already been given. This exception is concerned with attempts to violate a range or index constraint at run-time.

For example, if we have the declaration

  list : **array** (1 .. 20) **of** *integer*;

and an attempt is made to access the component *list*(21) then a *constraint_error* exception will be raised.

A *numeric_error* exception occurs when a numeric operation cannot give a correct result. The most common reason for this is an attempt to divide by zero.

If we try to leave a function other than by a return statement a *program_error* exception is raised, whereas if we get stuck in an infinite series of recursive calls and eventually run out of storage space a *storage_error* exception will be raised.

Several other circumstances can lead to each of these exceptions being raised, but these are the situations which you are most likely to encounter.

The other exception which has already been described is the *data_error* exception. Unlike the other exceptions described here, this exception is not defined in package *standard*, but is made available through the package *student_io*. It is the means by which we can check that data being read has the correct type or is in the correct range. Handling this exception ourselves can allow us to recover from an attempt to read wrong data.

When data consists of both numeric and character items, it is surprisingly easy to make a mistake in the program or in the presentation of the data which results in the *get* statements and the data being read to go out of phase. This usually leads to an attempt to read a letter or punctuation character when a number is expected and so a *data_error* exception is raised.

Let us now see how we can handle such an exception for ourselves.

16.3 Handling exceptions

When information of the wrong type is typed into a program as data, we can either try to recover from the error by writing a special exception handler, or we can just let the system handle the exception for itself. This will result in the program being terminated. A specially written exception handler might, on the other hand, try to recover by rejecting the offending item and requesting the user to try again.

Let us assume that a particular problem requires whole numbers in the range 1 to 15 to be typed in as data and that we have a subtype declared as

> **subtype** *small_pos* **is** *positive* **range** 1 .. 15;

Two possible errors can occur when a data item is read. The item may not be in the correct range, or it may not be a whole number. In both cases a *data_error* exception will be raised.

Exception handlers are associated with a sequence of statements in what is called a "frame". A frame that has exception handlers always includes the construct

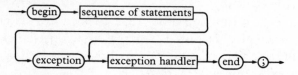

This construct can occur anywhere we can have a statement.

The following procedure contains a *data_error* exception handler within a loop. This allows further attempts to be made if the initial attempt to read a small positive integer number fails.

```
--frame starts here
procedure get_small(num : out small_pos) is
begin
   --read number in small_pos'range
   --if wrong data is read repeated attempts are made
   loop
      begin --inner frame starts here
         get(num);
         return;
      exception
         when data_error = >
            skip_line;
            put_line("small positive integer expected");
      end; --inner frame ends here
      put_line("try again");
   end loop;
end get_small;
--end of frame
```

The *data_error* exception handler is associated with the two statements

```
get(num);
return;
```

which occur between the reserved words **begin** and **exception** in the inner frame. No exception handlers are associated with the *get_small* procedure frame.

Let us now consider what happens when the body of procedure *get_small* is executed. The loop is entered and within the loop we enter the inner frame. The statement

   get(num);

is executed and if this is successful, i.e. if an integer in the range 1 to 15 is read, we continue on to the return statement which causes the procedure to be left. The loop and the exception handler have had no effect.

Let us now consider what happens if the statement

   get(num);

is not executed correctly but, due to an attempt to read erroneous data, a *data_error* exception is raised. When this happens normal execution of the statements in the inner frame is abandoned and control is transferred to the exception handler.

After the statements in the exception handler have been executed we leave the frame. The statement following the frame is

   put_line("try again");

This statement is executed and, because we are at the end of the loop, control is transferred back to its beginning, where another attempt is made to read the data item.

To see how this will work in practice, let us assume that we have two variables declared as

   a, b : small_pos;

and that we are to execute the statements

   put_line("two small positive numbers please");
   get_small(a); put_line("first number read successfully");
   get_small(b); put_line("second number read successfully");

In response to this, the data

   7, 12

is typed in.

The *get_small* procedure is entered and the value 7 is read and assigned to *num*. On leaving the procedure the variable *a* is given the value 7. We then enter procedure *get_small* for a second time. This time, when we attempt to execute

   get(num);

a comma is encountered. This causes a *data_error* exception to be raised. Normal execution of the inner frame is abandoned and control is transferred to the *data_error* exception handler. Procedure *skip_line* is called to skip all the remaining information on the input line, i.e. *skip_line* is called to clear up the mess left by the attempt to read wrong data. The error message

> small positive integer expected

is then output, after which we leave the frame, write the message

> try again

and return to the beginning of the loop.

We are now in a position to try again. If the number 12 is typed in, it will be successfully read and the procedure will be left with the variable *b* being given the value 12.

The dialogue with the computer has been

> two small numbers please
> 7, 12
> first number read successfully
> small positive integer expected
> try again
> 12
> second number read successfully.

after which *a* and *b* will have the values 7 and 12 respectively.

In this example the *data_error* exception was raised by the failure to correctly read an integer number, i.e. it was initially raised during execution of the *get* procedure. Although a subprogram or package body constitutes a frame, the *get* procedure did not handle the exception itself but passed it on to the frame containing the call of procedure *get*. It is often the case that a procedure cannot fully deal with an error which has occurred during its execution. What is then important is for it to transmit the fact that there has been an error, and say what the error is, to the frame containing the procedure call so that appropriate action may be taken there.

As an example of this let us again consider our stack handling procedures. When we wrote procedures *push* and *pop* we checked that no attempt was made to add an item to a full stack or remove an item from an empty stack. Instead of explicitly checking for these possibilities, we could have allowed the array index to go out of range and have picked up and dealt with the resulting *constraint_error* exception.

If we assume the declarations

```
type list is array (1 .. 100) of character;
type char_stack is
  record
    item : list;
    top : natural := 0;
  end record;
```

then the *pop* procedure can be written without error checks as

```
procedure pop(x : out character; stack : in out char_stack) is
begin
  --pop top character from the stack
  x := stack.item(stack.top);
  stack.top := stack.top − 1;
end pop;
```

If this procedure is called when *stack.top* has the value zero, normal execution of the procedure body will be abandoned when the attempt is made to access the array component *stack.item(stack.top)*. Because the procedure does not contain a *constraint_error* exception handler, the procedure body is left and the exception is again raised in the frame containing the offending call of procedure *pop*. A check is then made to see if there is an appropriate exception handler associated with the call. If there is not then that frame is abandoned.

Frames are abandoned in this way until a suitable exception handler is encountered or we return to the main program or the statements in a library package body. If no suitable handler is encountered the system deals with the exception and this usually means termination of the program.

Sometimes it is useful partially to process an exception within a frame before passing on information about it. This can be done by raising another exception during execution of the exception handler. A version of procedure *pop* could be written as

```
procedure pop(x : out character; stack : in out char_stack) is
begin
  --pop top character from the stack
  x := stack.item(stack.top);
  stack.top := stack.top − 1;
exception
  when constraint_error = >
```

```
        put_line("Stack is empty");
        raise constraint_error;
    end pop;
```

If a *constraint_error* exception is raised during execution of this version of *pop* then normal execution of the procedure is abandoned and the *constraint_error* exception handler entered. After the error message

    Stack is empty

has been printed another *constraint_error* exception is raised. The frame is then abandoned and the new exception is raised in the frame containing the procedure call.

If the exception had not contained a raise statement then this frame would have fully dealt with the exception and the frame in which the erroneous call had been made would not have been informed that an error had occurred. This is important because when a subprogram is abandoned the values of any **out** or **in out** parameters are not passed back to the calling routine as normal. It is therefore vital, at the point of call of procedure *pop*, to be informed whether the procedure has been executed successfully or has been abandoned.

We have only considered exceptions which have been raised during the execution of a statement. It is also possible for an exception to be raised during the elaboration of a declarative part. When entering a procedure for example, we might try to elaborate the object declaration

    number : *small_pos* := 16;

When an exception is raised during the elaboration of a declarative part, the current frame is immediately abandoned with no attempt being made to enter the local exception handler. Exception handlers may therefore safely assume that declarative parts have been fully elaborated and that all local variables have been allocated storage and, where appropriate, have been given initial values.

Now that we have seen several examples of exception handlers, let us look at their general form:

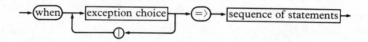

An exception choice is either the name of an exception or is the reserved word **others**. The **others** choice can only occur in the last of a sequence of exception handlers and it must be the only choice for that handler. As you would expect it caters for all exceptions which are not named explicitly.

16.4 Declaring exceptions

As we have seen, when we partially process an exception it is often useful to raise the same exception again. In such cases the exception does not have to be named and so our exception handler in procedure *pop* could be rewritten as

```
exception
    when constraint_error = >
        put_line("Stack is empty");
    raise;
```

A drawback of just passing on a predefined exception is that there are often several different reasons why it could be raised. An alternative is to declare a new exception such as, say,

```
stack_error : exception;
```

and to raise this exception in the exception handler:

```
exception
    when constraint_error = >
        put_line("Stack is empty");
    raise stack_error;
```

A frame containing a call of procedure *pop* can now contain both a *constraint_error* and a *stack_error* exception handler to deal separately with any error in manipulating the stack and a *constraint_error* exception which has been raised for some other reason.

Now that we know about exceptions we are in a position to write an improved stack package in which any errors in manipulating the stack will cause a *stack_error* exception to be raised.

The visible part of the package will become

```
package stack is
    --standard stack handling subprograms
    stack_error : exception;
    procedure push(x : character);
    procedure pop (x : out character);
    function stack_is_empty return Boolean;
    function stack_top return character;
    procedure reset_stack;
    end stack;
```

The contents of the package body are hidden from the units which use the package. All we need to know is that if any errors occur when we access the stack then a *stack_error* exception will be raised.

A possible implementation of procedure *push* is given below:

```
procedure push(x : character) is
begin
    --add character to stack
    st.top := st.top + 1;
    st.item(st.top) := x;
exception
    when constraint_error = >
        put_line("Stack is already full");
        raise stack_error;
end push;
```

Procedure *pop* and function *stack_top* can be modified in a similar way. The other declarations in the package body do not have to be changed from the version given in chapter 13.

16.5   Using exceptions

In the last chapter we wrote a program which used the stack package to help in converting an infix expression to reverse Polish. In that program we assumed that the infix expression was well-formed. Now that we know how to handle exceptions, let us extend the program so that it can deal with possible errors in the infix expression.

We must first consider the errors which can occur and how they can best be handled. The infix expression must begin and end with an operand, and operands and operators must alternate. This check can easily be performed by having a Boolean flag to indicate whether an operator or an operand is expected next. Open brackets can occur only where we can have operands and they must be followed by an operand. Close brackets can occur only where we can have an operator and they must be followed by an operator or be at the end of the expression.

Spaces can be ignored, but any other unexpected character must be reported as an error. The only other problem is unbalanced brackets. If we have too many open brackets they will still be on the stack when we come to the end of the expression. A test for this can easily be added to the program. Trying to deal with extra close brackets will result in an attempt to remove an item from an empty stack. This error can be handled by a *stack_error* exception handler.

A useful extension to the problem is to be able to deal with several infix expressions. Each expression to be converted will be on a new line, with the end of the sequence being indicated by a blank line. When we have a blank line the predefined function *end_of_line* returns the value *true* before any attempt has been made to read any characters from the line.

Let us now write the program. As well as our new stack package, it will again use package *convert*.

The top-level algorithm is

loop while the line is not blank
    convert infix expression to postfix and write the postfix
        expression
    get ready to deal with the next line
end loop

and the structure of the solution to the subproblem

convert infix expression to postfix

is basically unchanged from our earlier program.

PROGRAM 16.1

```
with student_io; use student_io;
with stack, convert; use stack, convert;
procedure rev_Polish is

    procedure infix_to_reverse_Polish is
        next_char : character;
        operator : op_char;
        operand_next : Boolean := true;
        --flag true if next_char is to be an operand
        order_error, spurious_error, bracket_error : exception;
        --stack operations declared in package stack
        --op_char and precedence declared in convert
    begin
        --convert the next infix expression to reverse Polish
        --stack assumed to be empty on procedure entry
        --it is always empty on exit
        while not end_of_line loop
            get(next_char);
            --deal with the different kinds of character
            case next_char is
            when 'a' .. 'z' | 'A' .. 'Z' = >
                if not operand_next then
                    raise order_error;
                end if;
                put(next_char); --operand written
                operand_next := false;
            when '+' | '-' | '*' | '/' = >
                if operand_next then
                    raise order_error;
                end if;
```

```
        loop
           exit when stack_is_empty or else
              precedence(next_char) > precedence(stack_top);
           pop(operator); put(operator);
        end loop;
        push(next_char);
        operand_next := true;
     when '(' = >
        if not operand_next then
           raise order_error;
        end if;
        push('(');
     when ')' = >
        if operand_next then
           raise order_error;
        end if;
        --pop operators up to and including '('
        loop
           pop(operator);
           exit when operator = '(';
           put(operator);
        end loop;
     when ' ' = >
        null;
     when others = >
           raise spurious_error;
     end case;
  end loop;
  --check that last character was an operand
  if operand_next then
     raise order_error;
  end if;
  --write remaining contents of stack
  while not stack_is_empty loop
     pop(operator);
     if operator = '(' then
        raise bracket_error;
     end if;
     put(operator);
  end loop;
  new_line;
exception
  when stack_error | bracket_error = >
     put_line("Unmatched brackets");
     reset_stack;
```

```
            when spurious_error = >
                 put_line("Spurious character encountered");
                 reset_stack;
            when order_error = >
                 put_line("Operators and operands in wrong order");
                 reset_stack;
         end infix_to_reverse_Polish;

      begin
         --read series of infix expressions and convert
         --them to reverse Polish
         --reading a blank line terminates the program
         while not end_of_line loop
            --stack is empty
            infix_to_reverse_Polish;
            --stack is again empty
            --get ready to process next line
            skip_line;
         end loop;
      end rev_Polish;
```

Because any error in the infix expression causes an exception to be raised, the handling of errors is kept away from normal execution of the program. This helps to keep the program easy to read and understand.

Procedure *infix_to_reverse_Polish* fully handles each of the exceptions and so the main program does not need to be informed that an error has occurred. In each handler a suitable error message is printed and the stack is then reset to empty, ready for the next expression. After an expression has been successfully converted, the stack will automatically be empty. Once the procedure has either been abandoned or left normally, procedure *skip_line* is called to read any remaining characters on the line plus the line terminator. In this way the program is properly positioned at the beginning of the next line to check if it is blank and if not to begin reading the next infix expression.

Exercises

1. Describe the difference between the handling of an exception when it is raised during the execution of a statement and when it is raised during the elaboration of a declarative part.
2. Complete the body of package *stack* described in section 16.4.
3. Modify Program 6.3 so that any errors in the data are handled by suitable exception handlers. After handling the error the program should be able to continue and deal with the next expression.

17

Files

17.1 Introduction

We saw in chapter 1 that information could be held on backing store, usually disks or magnetic tape, in what are called files. We shall refer to these files as "external files". If you have been running the Ada programs in this book on a computer, you will have been making extensive use of such files for, before we can translate and then run an Ada program, it must have been put into a file on backing store. This is done by typing the program into the computer as data to a special program called the editor. This editor program reads what we type in at a terminal and puts it into an external file.

If at a later date we wish to change an Ada program, we again use the editor. This time the editor reads the contents of the external file which contains the version of the program we wish to change, together with the proposed changes, which we type in at a terminal. These two pieces of information are then used to create an updated version of the program, which is put into a new external file.

Although we have used files to store Ada programs, we have assumed that, when a program is executed, the data for it is typed in at an interactive terminal and the results are displayed on a VDU screen. When we have a large amount of data it is inconvenient to have to type in all the data each time the program is run. A better approach would be to put some or all of the data into an external file on backing store. Our program will then be able to read data from this external file instead of from the terminal. The data will not have to be re-typed each time the program is run.

Similarly, instead of displaying all our results on the VDU screen we can write information to an external file. It is often the case that the results produced by a program are not intended for humans to read, but are to be used as data for another program. In such cases results are output to an external file so that they can be used as input data for the other program, or indeed be the input data for a later run of the same program.

Consider, for example, a program which is used each week to produce the pay cheques for a company's employees. Data for this program will come from two sources. One will be an external file containing all the past information about each employee. The other will be information about the work done by each employee in the current week. This information may also be in an external file or may be typed in at a terminal.

The result of running this program will be to print out the pay cheques for the employees together with statements showing how the pay has been calculated and how much has been deducted for tax, etc. A new file of information on each employee composed of information from the old file updated by the current week's information will also be produced. This new file, created during one run of the program, will be used as input data for the run the following week.

17.2 Reading from a file

Each external file on backing store can be referred to by a name which we shall call its external file name. The name conventions for files vary from one computer system to the next and have nothing to do with the Ada language. It is therefore not particularly convenient to refer in a program to a file by the string of characters which makes up its external name.

Within an Ada program we can declare objects to be of a built-in type called *file_type*, as in the declaration

> *weather_data, forecast* : *file_type*;

If we wish to read information from, or write information to, a file we specify which file we want by referring to an object of type *file_type*. A *file_type* object is associated with a particular external file by special procedures which are made available to us through the library package *student_io*.

Let us now look at how this is done. We shall assume that we have one or more files on backing store which contain at least 50 integers. We are going to write a procedure to read and find the sum of the first 50 integers in such a file.

The outline algorithm is

> open the file so that it can be read
> set the running total to zero
> loop 50 times

>   read the next integer from the file
>   add it to the running total
>   end loop
>   close the file

The procedure will require two parameters; the name of the external file, which will be a string of characters; and an **out** parameter of type *integer* to return to the calling program the result of adding together the 50 integers.

We can read only from a file which has been given the "file mode" *in_file* and we can write only to a file which has been given the file mode *out_file*. These two file modes are the literals of the predefined enumeration type *file_mode*, which has been defined behind the scenes as

>   **type** *file_mode* **is** (*in_file, out_file*);

This is used in the following procedure along with two new predefined procedures *open* and *close*.

>   **procedure** *read_fifty*(*external_name* : *string*;
>   *total* : **out** *integer*) **is**
>   *numbers_file* : *file-type*;
>   *value* : *integer*;
>   *sum* : *integer* := 0;
>   **begin**
>   --read and sum the first 50 integers in the file
>   *open*(*numbers_file*, *in_file*, *external_name value*);
>   **for** *i* **in** 1 .. 50 **loop**
>   *get*(*numbers_file*, *value*);
>   *sum* := *sum* + *value*;
>   **end loop**;
>   *close*(*numbers_file*);
>   *total* := *sum*;
>   **end** *read_fifty*;

The first statement in procedure *read_fifty*

>   *open*(*numbers_file*, *in_file*, *external_name*);

causes the *file_type* object *numbers_file* to be associated with the external file whose name is held in the string *external_name*, and for this file to be opened so that the information in it can be read.

Once we have opened a file we need a means of reading the information which it contains. In this chapter we assume that the files are what is known as "text files", i.e. that they are files of characters organised into lines. This is exactly the form in which the information is written to a VDU screen or is typed in at a terminal, and we use overloaded versions of the *get*, *put* and other subprograms which we have been using up till now.

When the statement

> *get(value)*;

is executed, an integer is read from the "standard input device", which we have assumed to be an interactive terminal. To read the integer from the external file which has been associated with *numbers_file* we use the procedure call

> *get(numbers_file, value)*;

Similarly overloaded versions of other procedures and functions are available through *student_io*. We shall meet most of them shortly.

Once procedure *read_fifty* has read the 50 numbers from the file and calculated their sum, the external file associated with *numbers_file* is closed by the procedure call

> *close(numbers_file)*;

This call breaks the association between the external file and the *file_type* object *numbers_file*. We then leave procedure *read_fifty*.

If an external file called *peoples_ages* existed on backing store and contained the ages of 50 people, and we wished their sum to be put into an integer variable *sum_ages*, this would be achieved by the call

> *read_fifty("peoples_ages", sum_ages)*;

Note that the name of the external file is passed over as a string.

If we had another external file called *stock_holding* and we wished the first 50 integers in it to be summed and the result stored in an integer variable called *total_stock*, this would be achieved by the call

> *read_fifty("stock_holding", total_stock)*;

Our procedure can therefore be used with any external file which contains at least 50 integer numbers.

17.3 Creating and deleting files

Let us now consider another problem. We have an external file containing the names and exam results of 500 students. The information about each student is on two consecutive lines. The first line contains the student's name and the second his or her three exam results. We wish to create a new file which will contain the names and the average marks obtained by each of the 500 students. Once we have done this we wish to delete the external file containing the original exam results from the backing store. We can assume that no student name has more than 30 characters.

This problem can be solved by the following procedure:

```
procedure produce_averages(old_file, new_file : string) is
    exams, averages : file_type;
    exam_result, exam_total : natural;
    exam_average : real;
    name : string(1 .. 30);
    name_length : natural := 0;
begin
    open(exams, in_file, old_file);
    create(averages, out_file, new_file);
    for students in 1 .. 500 loop
        --read name and results from the next two lines of the file
        get_line(exams, name, name_length);
        exam_total := 0;
        for exam in 1 .. 3 loop
            get(exams, exam_result);
            exam_total := exam_total + exam_result;
        end loop;
        skip_line(exams);
        exam_average := real(exam_total) / 3.0;
        --write name and average on the same line
        put(averages, name(1 .. name_length));
        put(averages, exam_average); new_line(averages);
    end loop;
    delete(exams); close(averages);
end produce_averages;
```

This procedure uses overloaded versions of several procedures which we have met before, namely *put*, *get_line*, *skip_line* and *new_line*. When a file is not specified in a call of the *put* or *new_line* procedures the information is written to the "standard output device", which we have assumed to be the VDU screen. When a file is specified the information is instead written to that file.

If the exam results are in an external file called *class_results* and we want the averages to go into a new file called *student_averages*, a suitable call of this procedure would be

```
produce_average("class_results", "student_averages");
```

Let us now follow the action of this procedure. First the external file called *class_results* is opened for reading and is associated with the *file_type* object called *exams*. Then a new external file called *student_ averages* is created and is associated with the *file_type* object called *averages*.

The names and results in the external file associated with *exams* are then read and the 500 names and averages are written to the external file associated with *averages* by repeatedly executing the procedure calls

> *put(averages, name(1 .. name_length))*;
> *put(averages, exam_average)*; *new_line(averages)*;

Once all the exam averages have been written to this new file, the file associated with *exams* is deleted, i.e. the external file *class_results* is deleted from backing store. The newly-created file called *student_ averages* is then closed.

As you might expect, exceptions are raised if any of these file handling procedures are used incorrectly. If we try to open or create a file which is already open, or if we try to close or delete a file which has not been opened, then a *status_error* exception is raised. The current status of a file can be checked by means of the Boolean function *is_ open*, as in the statement

> **if** *is_open(averages)* **then**
> > *close(averages)*;
> **end if**;

If the string of characters used to identify the external name of a file has the wrong form, or if we try to open an external file which does not exist, then a *name_error* exception is raised. If we try to open, create or delete a file for which we do not have permission to do these things, then a *use_error* exception is raised.

A *mode_error* exception is raised if we try to read from a file which is not in file mode *in_file* or if we try to write to a file which is not in file mode *out_file*. We can find the current mode of a file by calling the predefined function *mode*. It has one parameter of type *file_type* and returns a value of type *file_mode*.

17.4 Copying a file

When an object of type *file_type* is declared, we do not have to specify how large the file is. So file handling procedures must be written such that they can deal with files of any length. This means that when the contents of a file is being read there must be some means of indicating when we have come to the end. This is achieved by the predefined function *end_of_file*, which is analogous to *end_of_line* and is true when we have read to the end of the file and is false otherwise.

It is used in the following procedure, where the contents of one file are copied to another with the line structure being preserved:

```
procedure copy(old_file, new_file : string) is
    ch : character;
    source, destination : file_type;
begin
    --copy contents of source to destination
    open(source, in_file, old_file);
    create(destination, out_file, new_file);
    loop
      exit when end_of_file (source);
      if end_of_line(source) then
        skip_line(source);
        new_line(destination);
      else
        get(source, ch);
        put(destination, ch);
      end if;
    end loop;
    close(source); close(destination);
  end copy;
```

As has already been said, text files are organised as lines of characters. In fact, groups of lines are organised into pages and there is a procedure *new_page* whose action is to terminate the current line if this has not already been done and then to write a page terminator. Similarly, there is a procedure *skip_page* which will skip the rest of the current page in the same way that *skip_line* will skip the rest of the current line.

Each text file is terminated by a line terminator, followed by a page terminator which is then followed by a file terminator. The function *end_of_file* becomes true when this sequence of line, page and file terminator is encountered or when a file terminator is encountered.

When we have been writing to a file and we call procedure *close*, it ensures that the file is properly terminated with the appropriate line, page and file terminators. If we try to read past the end of a file the exception *end_error* is raised.

Exercises

1. Write a procedure which will take the contents of two files and will create a third file consisting of the first file followed by the contents of the second file.

2. We have two files, each of which contains integer numbers in non-decreasing order. Write a procedure to merge the information in these two files into a third file. Hence if the first file contained the numbers

    3 19 467 467 543

    and the second file contained the numbers

    7 19 219

    then the new file will contain

    3 7 19 19 219 467 467 543

3. Modify your answer to question 2 so that your newly-created merged file will contain no duplicates.

4. Two societies each have names of their members on file in alphabetic order. The two societies are to amalgamate and you have been asked to design and write a procedure which will read the membership lists from the two membership files and create a new amalgamated membership file in which the names of the members are still in alphabetic order. You may assume that no person is a member of both societies.

5. Temperatures have been collected from a remote weather station over the last year and have been written to a file on backing store. The file contains the minimum and maximum temperature, and the temperature at noon for each day of the year, starting with 1 January.
    Determine which day of the year had

    (iii) the lowest temperature,
    (ii) the highest temperature,
    (iii) the highest noon temperature.

    Which month had, on average, the lowest minimum, and which had the lowest maximum daily temperature?

APPENDIX 1

The reserved words

Because this book does not cover the whole of the Ada language, not all the Ada reserved words have been mentioned in the text. A complete list is given below.

abort	else	new	select
abs	elsif	not	separate
accept	end	null	subtype
access	entry		
all	exception	of	task
and	exit	or	terminate
array		others	then
at	for	out	type
	function		
begin		package	use
body	generic	pragma	
	goto	private	when
case		procedure	while
constant	if		with
	in	raise	
declare	is	range	xor
delay		record	
delta	limited	rem	
digits	loop	renames	
do		return	
	mod	reverse	

APPENDIX 2

The package *student_io*

A library package called *text_io* is available with all Ada systems because its contents are part of the definition of the Ada language. All the file handling procedures and functions such as *open*, *create*, *delete*, etc. together with facilities for reading and writing characters and strings are defined in this package. The library package *student_io* used in this book uses all of these procedures and functions in exactly the same way as *text_io*.

The disadvantage of using package *text_io* directly in simple programs comes when we wish to read or write integer or real values. The overloaded versions of *get* and *put* used to read integer or real values are defined within *text_io* in what are known as "generic packages". Within *student_io*, on the other hand, these procedures are made directly available to the user in the same way as the *get* and *put* procedures for characters and strings.

It is likely that, when Ada is being used for teaching, a package similar to *student_io* will be available although it may well have a different name. If this is so then the context clause

    with *student_io*; **use** *student_io*;

will have to be changed to the name used on your local system.

If you are using an Ada system in which such a helpful package is not available then several additions have to be made to certain programs. The initial context clause should be changed to

    with *text_io*; **use** *text_io*;

and if a program is going to read or write integer values then the following declaration must be inserted at the beginning of the declarative part of the main procedure:

    package *int_io* **is new** *integer_io(integer)*; **use** *int_io*;

If real values are being used then the declaration

type *real* **is digits** 8;

is required and if real values are to be read or written we must have the declaration

package *real_io* **is new** *float_io(real)*; **use** *real_io*;

Once these declarations have been made, the rest of the program should work in exactly the same way as described in this book. These declarations are known as the "instantiation of a generic package" and you should now see why such a feature is best hidden from view until you have had a reasonable amount of experience.

APPENDIX 3

The ASCII character set

The 95 printable characters of the ASCII character set are given below as character literals. The ordering is that of their *pos* attribute, which is in the range 32 to 126. The value of *character'pos* (' ') is 32, *character'pos*('!') is 33 and *character'pos*(' ~') is 126.

' '	'!'	'"'	'#'	'$'	'%'	'&'	'''
'('	')'	'*'	'+'	','	'-'	'.'	'/'
'0'	'1'	'2'	'3'	'4'	'5'	'6'	'7'
'8'	'9'	':'	';'	'<'	'='	'>'	'?'
'@'	'A'	'B'	'C'	'D'	'E'	'F'	'G'
'H'	'I'	'J'	'K'	'L'	'M'	'N'	'O'
'P'	'Q'	'R'	'S'	'T'	'U'	'V'	'W'
'X'	'Y'	'Z'	'['	'\'	']'	'^'	'_'
'`'	'a'	'b'	'c'	'd'	'e'	'f'	'g'
'h'	'i'	'j'	'k'	'l'	'm'	'n'	'o'
'p'	'q'	'r'	's'	't'	'u'	'v'	'w'
'x'	'y'	'z'	'{'	'|'	'}'	'~'	

ANSWERS TO SELECTED EXERCISES

Chapter 2

6. A program can be created by modifying Program 2.2. The identifier *sum* could be changed to *difference* and the assignment statement to

    difference := *second* − *first*;

    Changes should also be made to the program name, the comments and the message printed.

Chapter 3

2. *integer, real, character* and *string*

5. (a) *number, size* : *integer*;
   (b) *first_in_alphabet* : **constant** *character* := 'a';
   (c) **type** *month* **is** (*Jan, Feb, March, April, May, June, July, Aug, Sep, Oct, Nov, Dec*);
   (d) *vacation* : *month*;
   (e) *first_month* : **constant** *month* := *Jan*;
   (f) *name* : **constant** *string* := "Robert Clark";
   (g) *zero* : **constant** *real* := 0.0;

Chapter 4

2. 53 59 75 212
   53.6 59.0 75.2 212.0

5. *first* > *second*
   first **rem** *second* = 0
   first >= 0 **and** *second* >= 0
   first > 0 **xor** *second* > 0
   first **in** 1 .. 6

6. The first set of statements will swap the values of *my_appointment* and *your_appointment* and the second will set them both equal to *wed*.

7. Note that a real expression must be used in the calculation and that 100 should be written as 100.0.

Chapter 5
5(iv)
```
with student_io; use student_io;
procedure adding is
  sum : real := 0.0;
  n : integer;
  plus_or_minus_one : real := 1.0;
begin
  get(n);
  for number in 1 .. n loop
    sum := sum + plus_or_minus_one / real(number);
    plus_or_minus_one := - plus_or_minus_one;
  end loop;
  put("sum = "); put(sum);
  new_line;
end adding;
```

7. Remember to guard against a possible infinite loop when income plus interest is greater than expenditure.

Chapter 6
3. The statement
```
  get (operator);
```
must be expanded to
```
  loop
    get(operator);
    exit when operator /= ' ';
  end loop;
```
Any spaces before the numbers will be skipped automatically.

Chapter 7
6.
```
procedure month(days_in_month : positive; start_day : day) is
  days_in_line : positive := 1;
begin
  put_line("  Su  M  Tu  W  Th  F  Sa");
  for blanks in mon .. start_day loop
    put("   ");
    days_in_line := days_in_line + 1;
```

```
        end loop;
    for days in 1 .. days_in_month loop
        put(days, width = > 5);
        if days_in_line = 7 then
            new_line;
            days_in_line := 1;
        else
            days_in_line := days_in_line + 1;
        end if;
    end loop;
    new_line;
end month;
```

Chapter 8

1. *four, four, queen, king, jack, two.*
None of the statements would cause *constraint_error* exceptions to be raised.

4. **subtype** *printable_character* **is** *character* **range** ' ' .. '˜';

Chapter 9

5.
```
type month is (Jan, Feb, March, April, May, June, July,
                Aug, Sep, Oct, Nov, Dec);
function day_in_year(this_month : month; this_day : positive)
        return positive is
    type days is array (month) of positive;
    --assume a leap year
    days_in_month : constant days := (31, 29, 31, 30, 31, 30,
                                      31, 31, 30, 31, 30, 31);
    day_count : natural := 0;
    month_count : month := month'first;
begin
    while month_count < this_month loop
        day_count := day_count + days_in_month(month_count);
        month_count := month'succ(month_count);
    end loop;
    return day_count + this_day;
end day_in_year;
```

Chapter 10

5. **subtype** *name* **is** *string*(1 .. 20);
   type *name_list* **is array**(*positive* **range** < >) **of** *name*;
   names : *name_list*(1 .. 100);
   The only changes required in procedure *selection_sort* are that
   the type of the parameter is changed from *any_list* to *name_list*
   and that *smallest* is declared to be of subtype *name*.

Chapter 11

4. Example procedures are

```
procedure deal_cards(all_cards : deck;
                     north, east, south, west : out hand) is
   card : positive := 1;
begin
   for round in hand'range loop
      north(round) := all_cards(card);
      east(round) := all_cards(card + 1);
      south(round) := all_cards(card + 2);
      west(round) := all_cards(card + 3);
      card := card + 4;
   end loop;
end deal_cards;

function aces_in_hand(dealt : hand) return natural is
   count : natural := 0;
begin
   for round in hand'range loop
      if dealt(round).value = ace then
         count := count + 1;
      end if;
   end loop;
   return count;
end aces_in_hand;
```

Chapter 13

3. The definition of *values* and the type of the formal parameter *x*
   must be changed, but no change is required in the code.

5. The only change required is in the body of *special_word* where
   the definition of *word_list* has to be changed.

Chapter 15

4. **package** *convert* **is**
   subtype *op_char* **is** *character* **range** $'(' \, .. \, '>';$
   precedence : **constant array**(*op_char*) **of** *natural* :=
   $\qquad ('(' => 1,$
   $\qquad '<' \mid '=' \mid '>' \; => 2,$
   $\qquad '+' \mid '-' \; => 3,$
   $\qquad '\star' \mid '/' \; => 4,$
   $\qquad ')' \mid ';' \mid '.' \mid '0' \, .. \, ';' \; => 0);$
   end *convert*;

   If we assume that only legal expressions have to be handled, then the only other change required is to extend the choices of operators in the case statement in procedure *rev_Polish* to

   when $'+' \mid '-' \mid '\star' \mid '/' \mid '<' \mid '=' \mid '>' \; =>$

Chapter 16

3. Program 16.1 should be used as the model for the extension to Program 6.3. Occurrences of the errors "division by zero" and "error in operator" should now be picked up as exceptions. *Data_error* and the programmer defined *order_error* exceptions should also be handled. The exception handlers should be in an inner frame as in the example in section 16.3.

Chapter 17

4. The following outline algorithm can be used:

   read the first name from each of the society files
   loop
       if name from society A < name from society B then
           output society A name
           if no more names in society A file then
               output remaining society B names and leave loop
           end if
           read next society A name
       else
           output society B name
           if no more names in society B file then
               output remaining society A names and leave loop
           end if
           read next society B name
       end if
   end loop

INDEX

215